DEEPER THAN MOTIVATION

DEEPER THAN

THAN

MOTIVATION

JOVAN GLASGOW

Deeper Than Motivation:
Rewire Your Beliefs, Break Your Patterns, Transform Your Life
© 2026 Jovan Glasgow

Published by KCE Press.
Dallas, TX.

Printed in the United States of America.
First edition 2026.

Cover and layout design by G Sharp Design, LLC.
www.gsharpmajor.com

ISBN 979-8-9953457-1-8 (paperback)
ISBN 979-8-9953457-0-1 (hardcover)
ISBN 979-8-9953457-2-5 (ebook)

In a time when many men walk through life in isolation, I count
myself eternally blessed to have a brother and a best friend.

You have walked with me through some of the darkest
seasons of my life—never judging me, but always reminding
me that my humanity does not disqualify my capacity.

Your loyalty, your presence, and your belief in me
helped shape the man I am still becoming.

I dedicate this book to my brother and my best friend, Yemi Oyegunle.

I am a better man because I did not have to walk this journey alone.

TABLE OF CONTENTS

INTRODUCTION

Y OU DIDN'T PICK up this book because life is perfect.

You picked it up because, somewhere between who you were told to be and who you know you could be, something stopped lining up.

Maybe you're the high performer everyone claps for, but you're exhausted in a way sleep doesn't fix. Maybe you're the quiet fighter, the one who keeps showing up, holding everything together for everyone else, wondering why the person who believes in you the least is the one you see in the mirror. Maybe you've done all the "right things"—read the books, listened to the podcasts, attended the conferences—yet the patterns underneath your life haven't really shifted. The scenery changed. The story didn't.

If any of that sounds familiar, I wrote this for you.

I've spent years standing on stages, coaching leaders, and sitting across from people who look like they're "doing well" while privately battling questions they don't feel safe to say out loud. People who are accomplished but empty. People who are gifted but stuck. People who are motivated, but still losing themselves in the process of trying to win.

Somewhere along the way, motivation became our favorite drug.

We love the high of a powerful moment. The rush of a keynote. The hype of a conference. The playlist that makes you feel like you can take on the world—until the song ends, the conference is over, the room empties, and you're back in your real life with the same fears, the same habits, the same beliefs you walked in with.

Motivation can move your feet. But it will not heal your foundation.

What I've learned—through my own failures, grief, divorce, financial strain, and the kind of private battles I'll talk about in these pages—is that you can't outrun what you refuse to outgrow. You can't outperform the story you secretly believe about yourself. You can't "grind" your way past shame. You can't hustle your way around unhealed patterns.

At some point, the work has to go deeper than motivation.

This book is not about making you more hyped. It's about helping you become more whole.

In **Part I: Rewire Your Beliefs,** we're going to talk about the thing most people never slow down to face: the story you've attached to your pain. The quiet narratives that whisper, "You're not enough," "You're too much," or "You're too late." We'll confront shame, not as a feeling you have from time to time, but as a lens that has been quietly editing how you see yourself, your past, and your future. We'll talk about why you can be talented and trapped at the same time—and what it really means to stop quitting on you.

In **Part II: Break Your Patterns,** we'll move from belief to behavior. We'll talk about "normal" and why the life you've normalized may not actually be healthy. We'll unpack why becoming is the work, how identity is formed, and why confidence has less to do with being loud and more to do with being aligned. You'll see how your patterns are not proof that you're broken—they're evidence of where your beliefs have been in charge.

And in **Part III: Transform Your Life,** we'll step into the external— the visible life everyone else sees. We'll challenge the metrics you've been using to measure success, and we'll talk about what it looks like to live with intention instead of autopilot. We'll walk through burnout, balance, habits, adversity, and how to stay connected to your fire when the spotlight is off and the pressure is on. Not in theory. In the real, messy places where your faith, your family, your calling, and your humanity collide.

I'm not writing as a man with all the answers. I'm writing as a man who has had to sit with his own shame. A man who has had to face the ways he performed for approval, minimized his own pain, and confused being needed with being known. A man who has had to learn—over and over—that you don't get to transformation by pretending you're already there.

So before we go any further, I want to ask you a question.

Not "What do you want to achieve?"
Not "What's your fiveyear plan?"
Not even "What are your goals?"

I want to ask you this:

Who are you becoming while you chase what you're chasing?

Because if the version of you on the other side of your dreams is more exhausted, more resentful, more disconnected from who you really are, then what you're calling "success" might actually be slow selfdestruction with good branding.

These pages are not here to shame you. They're here to interrupt you. To give you language for what you've been feeling but couldn't fully articulate. To help you separate who you are from what you've survived. To invite you into a different way of seeing yourself, your story, and your future.

You may not know it yet, but by the time you close this book, you will be confronted with a choice.

Not the kind of choice you make once and forget about, but the kind that changes how you move in every room you walk into, every relationship you build, and every opportunity you say yes or no to.

That journey doesn't start at the mountaintop. It starts right where you are, with an honest look at your story and a decision not to quit on the person in it.

So before we go anywhere else, I want you to sit with three simple words that changed everything for me: you made it.

PART ONE

REWIRE YOUR BELIEFS

CHAPTER ONE

DON'T QUIT ON YOU

THE MORNING I HEARD "YOU MADE IT"

I WAS ENJOYING one of the best sleeps of my life, in this deep state of REM, stretched out on a kingsize bed, air temperature set just right, blackout curtains blocking out the light from the parking lot, and the slight white noise that I use as a way to fully immerse myself in deep sleep. All of it was intruded upon by the sound of my alarm clock going off at 5:30 a.m.

That alarm clock, set by me to wake me up on time, mattered because today was not just another day. This was the day I was embarking on a keynote presentation I was genuinely excited to give. The evening prior, I had spent time hanging out with some professionals at a local winery, having just flown in from Dallas to Midland, Texas. I was getting to know the hearts and minds of the Midland–Odessa team of difference makers who put on this annual conference, and the day felt different.

I felt a weight and a responsibility to deliver a message that transcended just that moment, a message that could permeate their lives professionally while also seeping into the personal areas of their lives. I firmly believe that messages meant to transform people cannot stay isolated in one area. I don't know if it has been by design or by experience, but I have always believed in the power of impacting people personally and professionally.

I think the attempt to ignore the personal aspects of a person's life is one of the ways we unintentionally dehumanize people, believing they are robots or machines who can shut off who they are personally whenever they step into professional situations. Yes, I believe in the power of boundaries and in knowing how to compartmentalize as a skill and not as a personality trait, but I can't help, in these transformative moments where I'm keynoting, but speak not just to behavior, but to being.

That morning, I got up, went through my devotion, pulled up my computer with my black coffee, and began walking through my deck as I prepared for the keynote presentation. As I walked through my slides, I was moved—not just by the words that were going to be entrusted through me, but by what it took to get there. I couldn't help but sit there for a moment and reflect on my journey to that point, under many trials and obstacles, uncertainty, and overwhelming fear. The list could go on. All the things I had to work past in order to get to the point of being able to show up and use my gift to serve others.

It was as though I was walking through the slide deck when tears started to well up in my eyes, and I simply made a statement to myself: Jovan, you made it.

Not "made it" in the sense of how we commonly use that phrase, as if I had arrived at some destination where success was guaranteed and all my dreams had paid off. I don't necessarily believe that I am aiming for a place. More than anything, I am aiming in this life to achieve a state of knowing that I have fulfilled my assignment in time and that my Godgiven purpose has been lived out.

But for me, those three words—you made it—were about something else. They were about coming into the present moment and speaking to the reality that there were times when I couldn't pay my light bill, times when my phone was about to be cut off, times when I didn't know where my next meal was going to come from. They were about working through the uncertainties that come with entrepreneurship, especially entrepreneurship where you are focused on impacting the lives of others.

There were moments when I was so overwhelmed by the pressure I was under that I found myself wrestling with a deeper question: If I ever "make it," will there be anything left of me when I get there? That question carried weight, because we all have different definitions of what "making it" means.

For one person, making it might mean becoming something they've never seen modeled before. For another, it could mean achieving a goal, a position, a possession, or a level of prominence. For someone else, it might simply mean they didn't fall into the trap of becoming their circumstances.

Regardless of the definition, that moment of slowing down that morning mattered. Not being controlled by the past. Not having anxiety about the future. Truly embracing the power of the present.

WHAT IT REALLY MEANS TO QUIT ON YOU

Before we go further, I need to name the premise of this chapter, because it is more subtle than we think.

Most people think quitting on yourself happens in the moment you walk away—the day you resign, file the papers, shut down the business, hang up the dream. But quitting on you almost never starts there. Quitting on you begins the moment you decide that what happened to you is who you are, instead of allowing what you've been through to shape who you are becoming.

You don't quit on you when life gets hard. You quit on you when you look at what life has handed you and say, "This is all I'll ever be." You quit on you when you allow disappointment to become your definition, when you let circumstances sit in the seat where identity should live.

This chapter is about refusing to let that happen.

THE POWER OF THE PRESENT MOMENT

As I got dressed that morning to head into what I would consider to be a battlefield—an interesting word to use, because for me I'm not battling people, I'm battling their beliefs—the beliefs, insecurities, inadequacies, perceptions, unconscious biases, and all the things that can create blocks to me articulating my message in a way that allows them to receive it, to let it move from head to heart and eventually to hands, I couldn't shake the revelation I'd had that morning: you made it.

My bio was read. The crowd stood and applauded as they introduced the keynote speaker, Jovan Glasgow. Before I even got into my time, I had to slow the room down. I simply started with this simple but significant thought: today is a new day.

"Today is a new day" is powerful, because it's not simply the turn of a day on our calendar. "Today is a new day" means that possibility is still possible. It means that I have another opportunity to overcome my greatest opposition. It means that I may not be there yet, but I'm on the way. It means that I'm not my history and I can still shift my legacy.

"Today is a new day" means that while most people are making the choice to resort to their backup plan, I'm making the decision to get back up.

"Today is a new day" is everything.

And not only is today a new day, but I had to take a moment to remind the room of something else: you made it.

You made it trying.
You made it crying.
You made it fighting.

You made it clawing.
You made it doubting.
You made it scared.
You made it set back.

You made it.

The reason I wanted to start there was because I wanted to highlight something we often diminish: the power of the present moment. Regardless of what has happened to you up to this point, you made it through another moment, another day, another opportunity where you still have time and space to take the pieces of your life and create something meaningful.

EVIDENCE OF STRENGTH, NOT A CONSOLATION PRIZE

I don't know your story up to this point. I don't know how your life has unfolded. I don't know what has been demanded of you, what it has cost you, or what has been happening beneath the surface. I don't know what you've had to manage quietly while still showing up for everyone else. But what I do know is this: you made it.

You may have made some mistakes, but you made it. You may not always have made the right decisions, but you made it. You may not be where you want to be, but you're not where you used to be. You made it.

And if you can acknowledge that, you begin to see that it is possible for your tomorrow to still look completely different than your yesterday. Sometimes making it is not a consolation prize. It is simply evidence of your strength.

Can I go a bit deeper?

As I continue to mature in my life and go through different experiences, I've realized that making it doesn't always mean that you're showing up to fight. As I've gotten more mature, I've realized that sometimes just showing up is the fight. Sometimes just getting out of bed is the win. Sometimes just putting on your clothes, doing your hair, getting a haircut, or trying again is the win.

We live in a culture that only celebrates outcomes. We clap for promotions, milestones, titles, and visible wins, but we rarely acknowledge endurance. We don't pause long enough to honor the resolve it takes to keep going when life didn't turn out the way we planned. We overlook the quiet resilience of people who kept showing up even while they were unsure, tired, or wrestling privately with questions they didn't yet have answers to.

There are seasons when simply staying in the fight is the victory. Seasons where survival is not weakness, but courage in its rawest form.

WHEN WE BECOME WHAT HAPPENED TO US

I don't want to spend this entire chapter recounting adversities, but I do want to levelset something important. As you think about the fact that you made it, here's where I'm going with this: it's easy to go through a process. It's another thing entirely to become the process you've gone through.

What I've recognized is that most people who have gone through something that could actually be beneficial for them, if they could harness it correctly, have lacked the ability to do so simply because they've become it.

This looks like a person who has gone through financial loss and, instead of using that loss as a way to gain a greater level of financial wisdom, allows themselves to believe that because they lost things financially, they can never rebound in that area. Or a person who has been through a divorce and cannot use that divorce as a way to become better at the most important relationships they have—their relationship with God and their relationship with themselves—so they can discover who they really are outside of titles and expectations.

It looks like a person who failed in business and now believes they were never created to be a good businessperson, when the truth is that failure on one level often precedes success on another.

You see, it's so easy for us to become the thing that has happened to us instead of allowing the thing that happened to become the catalyst for who we are becoming. This is one of the core ideas of not quitting on you.

And a shift that's going to be necessary for you to come out of this challenging season without becoming the season you're in is having an accurate lens—an accurate perspective—on the difference between who you are and what you've gone through.

I've come to believe that many people don't struggle because they lack ability or potential. They struggle because of what they start believing about themselves when things don't work out.

The real danger is not adversity itself. The real danger is the story we attach to it.

I firmly believe that however you define a thing is exactly what it will become, and ultimately what you will behold. Whatever you normalize, you rationalize. Whatever you rationalize, you actualize. When disappointment lingers long enough, it becomes a whisper that creates narratives about our worth, our capacity, and our future.

If we're not careful, we don't just experience difficulty. We internalize it. And when we internalize it long enough, it becomes a part of our identity.

That's why this chapter isn't about quitting on goals, ambitions, or dreams. It's about something far more personal. It's about not quitting on yourself.

A SOUTH KOREAN GRANDMOTHER AND THE THRESHOLD OF QUITTING

As much as I thought I understood the principle of not quitting, my threshold was challenged the day I heard about a South Korean woman whose story felt almost unbelievable.

Her name was Cha Sasoon. According to the reports, at the age of 65 she decided that she wanted to get her driver's license. She had a why. Her purpose, based on what was shared, was simple but powerful. She wanted to be able to travel. She wanted to take her grandchildren around. She wanted to go to the markets and do the things she wasn't able to do without having a vehicle.

So she made the decision at 65 years old to pursue it.

Here's where the story takes an interesting turn.

Cha Sasoon failed her driver's license test 960 times before she passed.

I still can't fully wrap my mind around that number. I'm a very visual person, so I can't help but imagine what it must have been like to be an employee at the DMV, watching Cha Sasoon walk in on day one with a big smile, excited to take her driver's license test for the very first time. I imagine her taking the test, coming back with a failure, and still holding onto a positive attitude, thinking to herself that it didn't happen the first time, but she could try again.

I also imagine being that DMV employee, encouraging her to give it another shot, believing for her that something would eventually shift.

But then I start thinking beyond the first few attempts. I imagine try number 7. Try number 120. Try number 276. Try number 465. Try number 832. Try number 910.

I want you to imagine with me what it would have been like to be in that DMV, seeing this woman show up over 959 times before she finally passed.

Can you imagine the scrutiny? The judgment? The questions people must have asked? The internal conversations she likely had to manage? The fear someone might have felt thinking, What if she does pass one day and we have to be on the same road together?

And yet, in the middle of all of that, she refused to quit. She didn't just push through the failure—she refused to become the failure.

What makes this story so significant to me is that I don't believe Cha Sasoon was focused on how many times she failed. I believe the only thing she was focused on was the fact that she hadn't succeeded yet.

This story changed my threshold for what I believe is acceptable when it comes to quitting.

She wanted freedom. She wanted to be able to take her grandchildren where they needed to go. She wanted more life. And because of that, failure did not have the authority to define her.

What makes her story remarkable is not simply that she eventually succeeded. It's how long she was willing to keep going.

Cha Sasoon passed her driving test after 960 attempts.

That number has stayed with me because it forces an uncomfortable reflection. Imagine showing up to the same place, hearing "no" again and again, and still deciding to return. Imagine the opinions, the discouragement, and the internal dialogue she must have had to navigate. Most of us would have stopped long before that. Not necessarily because we couldn't continue, but because we would have interpreted failure as a signal to quit.

But she didn't.

And the reason she didn't is important. Her pursuit wasn't driven by ego. It wasn't about proving anything to anyone. It was anchored in purpose. When purpose is clear, rejection loses its power to define you. When the "why" is strong enough, the "no" becomes information, not a verdict.

That story isn't about driving. It's about resolve. It's about the capacity human beings have to keep showing up when something matters deeply to them.

And it raises a question worth sitting with.

If someone can fail hundreds of times and still show up for a driver's license, how many times is too many when it comes to showing up for your peace? For your healing? For your relationships? For the life you're trying to build?

Most people don't quit because they're incapable. They quit because they begin to see themselves through the lens of disappointment. They stop separating what happened from who they are.

There's a critical distinction between making a mistake and believing you are one. Between falling short and concluding that you are short on value.

Your worth was never meant to be negotiated based on outcomes.

CIRCUMSTANCES, STANCE, AND IDENTITY

Your value is not contingent on your circumstances. It is not defined by what you have, what you've lost, how fast you're moving, or how others perceive your progress. You are valuable because you exist. And when you forget that, you give circumstances permission to tell you who you are.

This is where many people get trapped. They allow their environment, their finances, their failures, or their past to shape their identity. But circumstances were never meant to be the authority over your life. They are temporary conditions, not permanent definitions.

When we break the word circumstance down, it reveals something powerful. "Circum" refers to a cycle, something that surrounds or repeats. "Stance" speaks to posture, position, and identity.

In other words, your circumstance is simply your stance in a cycle.

If you allow what's happening around you to determine who you are, you will always feel controlled by it. But when you are grounded in your stance—your values, your identity, your sense of worth—you begin to realize that circumstances don't have the final say.

I like to say it this way: when you're bold in your stance, you cannot be controlled by your circumstance.

This is a powerful mindset shift, because you will never become what you can't see. And if your only vision and sight are external, you're not truly focused on who you have the potential and power to be internally.

Here's what I mean by that. Many of us can't change our circumstances immediately, but what we can do is change ourselves. And we can do that right now. We can do that in any moment.

We don't make a change in our circumstances by attempting to change the circumstances first. We make a change in our circumstances by changing ourselves. That is what we can control.

The moment you allow your circumstances to define you, you will always shrink to what is happening around you instead of rising to the power of what is occurring within you.

I've lived this tension personally.

I have stood on stages speaking hope and belief while privately navigating financial strain. I have been on stage speaking a positive message with a negative bank account, telling people they could chase their dreams while Chase was chasing me for overdraft fees.

I have encouraged others to pursue purpose while dealing with pressures that didn't align with the message I was delivering. I've shown up in moments pouring into the lives of others while sometimes feeling like I was operating on empty.

And in those moments, I had to make a decision. Would I allow my circumstances to rewrite my identity, or would I remain anchored in who I knew myself to be?

It's easy to mislabel this tension as imposter syndrome, but there's a thin line between imposter syndrome and identity sabotage. Imposter syndrome is often rooted in perfection, the belief that we need to be flawless to belong. Identity sabotage happens when we begin to believe that we are our circumstances.

Circumstances are simply a manifestation of behavior and environment. They are not a reflection of identity.

Circumstances change when people change first, not the other way around. And that realization is what I want to invite you into as we move forward from here. This journey begins with taking ownership of who you are so that you can become who you were created to be. And the first stage of that journey is awareness.

SHAME, REFLECTION, AND GROWTH

Awareness is something I'm going to talk to you about through the power of reflection. Reflection is a dynamic tool, and most of us are familiar with it in theory, but very few of us have learned how to do it well. Reflection is often where internal work begins, but it must be handled with care, because reflection can either become a source of clarity or a source of shame. Both involve looking back, but they produce very different outcomes.

Reflecting for clarity allows us to ask honest questions without condemning ourselves. It helps us identify patterns, assess choices, and recognize where alignment may have been lost. When reflection is rooted in clarity, it produces confidence. Confidence then creates influence, and influence creates impact. Reflection done well moves us forward.

Reflection done poorly does the opposite.

Reflecting from a place of shame turns reflection into selfattack. It becomes a form of punishment. Instead of learning from the past, we replay it. Instead of extracting wisdom, we extract condemnation. Shame keeps us stuck, cycling through what went wrong without giving us access to what can be redeemed.

Let me say this clearly, because it matters: clarity produces confidence, but shame produces paralysis.

At this point in my life, I've spent countless hours in conversations, coaching sessions, and rooms filled with leaders, professionals, and individuals from all walks of life. I've worked with thousands of people across different ages, stages, backgrounds, belief systems, and industries. And because I'm always focused on root cause, I'm constantly asking myself what patterns keep showing up, regardless of context.

What I'm about to say might surprise you, but in my experience, the greatest barrier to growth is not fear. It's not a lack of discipline. It's not a lack of confidence, communication ability, or resources. I've seen people grow with very little and stay stuck with a lot.

The greatest barrier to growth I've seen is shame.

Shame is the graduated version of guilt. Guilt says, "I did something wrong." Shame says, "Because I did something wrong, I am something wrong." And when shame takes root, it causes us to hide. As human beings, I can promise you one thing: none of us are perfect. I've never met a perfect person, and if I ever do, I've likely just met a liar.

The reason shame is so destructive to growth is because growth requires us to embrace the full picture. To grow, you have to be willing to see who you are, where you are, how you got there, what's standing in your way, what you do well, and where you struggle. You have to embrace both your strengths and your shortcomings, your gifts and your gaps, your potential and your problems.

And it's important to understand that embrace does not mean approval. Embrace means awareness.

But shame convinces us to hide parts of ourselves. And when we hide, reflection becomes distorted. We avoid truth instead of engaging it. And when we avoid truth, we rob ourselves of revelation. Awareness never grows in hiding.

You don't heal by punishing yourself into change. You heal by telling yourself the truth without condemnation.

One of my favorite scriptures says it this way: the truth will set you free. But truth can only free what you are willing to confront. Growth begins when you stop running from what's been chasing you internally and start facing it with honesty and grace.

WHY YOU CAN'T QUIT ON YOU

None of this can be achieved if you have already made the decision to quit on yourself.

As you move forward, I want you to hear this clearly. Do not quit on you. Not because the path is easy. Not because success is guaranteed. But because you are worth the fight. And for some of us, we've never heard those words used in the same sentence—you and worth.

Some of us have never believed that we are valuable apart from the value we produce. Some of us have never believed that our lives matter, that we have purpose, or that we bring something meaningful into this world. But this world only becomes better when people become the solutions to the problems that exist within it.

And if you quit on you, none of that journey can ever be completed. None of the impact can ever be realized. Whether quitting on yourself happens physically, mentally, emotionally, or spiritually, quitting on you always looks the same. It's the moment you allow life to simply happen to you instead of choosing to live in a way that allows life to happen through you.

I often think about the interconnectedness of life. How a paramedic saving a stranger, a doctor performing a lifechanging surgery, or a firefighter pulling a child out of a burning home can alter the entire trajectory of someone else's life in a single moment.

These people are strangers until the moment they become the reason someone else gets another chance.

And I can't help but wonder what would happen if any one of them had quit.

What's on the other side of you choosing not to become what happened to you, but instead allowing what happened to become fuel for what can happen through you? What would be possible if, regardless of the hell you've been through, you got up today, wiped the tears from your eyes, looked in the mirror, and said these words with conviction and clarity:

I made it. *And now it's time to make something meaningful out of my life.*

CHAPTER TWO

THE PARADOX OF REFLECTION

MOVING FROM THE Caribbean islands to America was a beautiful transition for me, and I must admit, one that brought with it a number of complexities. Some of the things that are considered normal in U.S. culture can feel abnormal when you grow up in the Caribbean.

I came from Antigua at the age of nineteen to pursue an education. My parents sent me to what they believed was the best place for a young man navigating identity and puberty—South Beach, Miami, Florida. Interestingly enough, most people don't know that I went to school for aeronautical science, focused on pursuing a degree in aeronautical engineering and avionics.

I grew up around planes. My mom worked in the airline industry for nearly two decades, and because of that, I developed a deep passion for aviation—one that I still carry to this day. A fun fact about me is that I am most focused, most relaxed, and most aligned when I'm in the air. There's something about being forty thousand feet above the ground, surrounded by clouds, with the sound of the engine gently rumbling, that allows me to disconnect from the constant connectivity of life—the expectations, the phone calls, the notifications.

In the air, I can access a level of focus that I struggle to reach on the ground.

Coming from the Caribbean islands, there were many cultural differences to navigate. Differences in expectations, differences in laws, differences in rules. One of the things that stood out to me almost immediately was the difference in driving norms.

In the Caribbean, you get your driver's license at the age of eighteen. Here in America, that age is sixteen. Not only that, but in the Caribbean we drive on the left-hand side of the road, with the steering wheel on the right-hand side of the car. In America, it's the inverse. We drive on the right-hand side of the road, and the steering wheel is on the left-hand side of the car.

Needless to say, after landing in America and getting acclimated to some of the new laws, I had to go get my driver's license so I could move back and forth to campus, handle life outside of school, and—if I'm being honest—maybe go to a few parties, but we'll leave that part out.

I remember passing my driver's license test, and thank God I wasn't in a situation like Cha Sa-soon from the *Don't Quit on You* chapter. It only took me one attempt, not nine hundred and sixty. I remember the feeling of receiving my driver's license here in the United States, knowing I was stamped and approved to embark on the highways and byways of life in the land of the free.

Even though I went through the test and passed the written exam, it's interesting to realize that nobody followed me around afterward to make sure I didn't revert to my old norms—like pulling out of Target and driving on the left-hand side of the road, which I may or may not have done a few times early on. But I'm not going to keep spending time writing down my sins.

I still remember buying my first car here in the United States. It was a 1996 Honda Civic. I bought it for about two thousand dollars, and to me, it felt like I had just purchased a Lamborghini. It was dark gray, had some average rims, but I wasn't worried, because I had plans for that car. I called it the *HondaGhini*, and I was determined to get it styled just the way I wanted.

Weeks later, I remember taking whatever money I could scrape together to start buying parts for that vehicle. And man, I loved that car. There's something about driving your first car that makes you feel like an adult, that makes you feel like a man.

Of course, I didn't love the insurance, the gas, the maintenance, or the tires—which is usually where we find ourselves loving the idea of getting the thing but rejecting what it actually takes to manage the thing we want. But that's a story for another day.

I remember coming back to campus one day from the local McDonald's, where I had just bought a Big Mac, some fries, and a Powerade. I was excited to get back to campus to eat. As I drove, I approached this large red sign on the right-hand side of the road that I had seen many times before. Four letters. One word.

STOP.

I had driven past that sign countless times in my life. And over time, I started to notice a pattern. Every time I stopped at that sign, nothing really happened. I would stop, pause for a moment, and then keep driving. So on this particular day, I made a decision. Instead of coming to a complete stop, I rolled through it.

No big deal. Or so I thought.

Because as I rolled through that sign, pressed the accelerator, and got back up to speed, the peace of the reggae vibes playing through my CD deck—yes, cars used CDs back then—was suddenly interrupted by a sharp punch in the atmosphere.

A siren.

And without even looking in my rearview mirror, I knew without a shadow of a doubt that it wasn't an ice cream truck. It wasn't the President of the United States stopping by the university to greet me. It wasn't an ambulance or a fire truck.

It was the police.

Without even needing to confirm it, I knew that siren was for me. And so I did what we all instinctively do in moments like that. I looked up into my rearview mirror. Just like I suspected, red and blue lights filled the glass behind me. "Miami-Dade" stretched across the hood of the patrol car, and through the speakers I heard a calm but firm voice telling me to pull over to the right.

I had seen plenty of movies where cops pulled people over. One of my favorite shows at the time was actually *Cops*. And for a brief moment, my imagination got the best of me. I thought about dropping a gear, hitting the gas, taking off, maybe getting closer to campus, letting the car roll in neutral, jumping out, and clearing the fence. None of that was real, of course—it was just the chaos of a young mind fueled by too much television and not enough wisdom.

So I did the only reasonable thing. I pulled over.

The officer stepped out of his vehicle and walked up to my window. Calm. Direct. "Driver's license and registration," he said. I handed them over. He looked at me and asked the question every guilty person dreads: "Do you know why I pulled you over?"

And like most people who know exactly what they did wrong, I responded honestly. I said, "I believe you pulled me over because I failed to stop at the stop sign."

He nodded. "Absolutely."

I immediately began apologizing, hoping that somehow my sincerity might earn me a little leniency. He listened, then said, "Wait right here. I'll be right back."

As I sat there in the car, what felt like eternity passed in my mind. Thoughts started racing. Maybe he's going to run my license and realize I pulled out of Target driving on the left-hand side of the road. Maybe he's going to do a random search and find something illegal in the trunk that I didn't even know was there from the previous owner. All kinds of irrational scenarios ran through my head, because again—I watched way too much TV.

I kept looking into the rearview mirror, waiting for whatever was going to happen next.

Eventually, the officer stepped out of his vehicle and walked back toward my car. In his hand was a piece of paper that looked suspiciously like a receipt from Walmart. I had given him my license and registration, but this was something else entirely.

He handed it to me and said, "This is your ticket; you'll need to pay it. And moving forward, make sure you come to a complete stop at stop signs. Have a great day."

The first words out of my mouth were, "Thank you."

I'm still not entirely sure why I thanked him for giving me a ticket, but I did. I put the car in drive and pulled away like the most responsible driver to ever exist.

Two hundred and thirty-eight dollars.

That was the cost of failing to stop at a stop sign.

From that day forward, every time I passed that stop sign, I caught myself looking back into the rearview mirror. Sometimes I would come to a stop for longer than ten seconds, just sitting there, scanning behind me, even though I was now fully obeying the rules.

And I wish I could tell you that this behavior lasted for a day or two. But it didn't. For months, I kept doing the same thing. I kept looking back. I kept bracing myself. I kept anticipating consequences that had already been paid for.

Even though I was no longer breaking the rules, I was still driving as if I was.

I hadn't come to the realization yet that reflecting on that moment—looking back in the rearview mirror—was never meant to be about reliving the guilt of what I had done. It was meant to teach me how not to repeat the mistake in the future.

Instead, I was looking back with shame. With embarrassment. With fear. And because of that, the past kept showing up in my present even though it no longer had authority there.

We've all heard the saying that there's a reason the rearview mirror is smaller than the windshield—that we're meant to spend more time looking forward than looking back. And while that sounds creative, the truth is, if the rearview mirror were the same size as the windshield, we wouldn't be able to see forward at all.

But here's the real point.

It's not the act of looking back that makes the difference. It's the posture by which we look back.

So many of us are moving forward in our lives while constantly glancing behind us—not to reflect with gratitude or learn with clarity, but to rehearse fear, guilt, and shame tied to mistakes we've already paid for. We experience the guilt of making a mistake, but then we look back with fear, and fear slowly turns that mistake into an identity.

We don't just say, "I made a mistake." We start believing, "I *am* the mistake."

I believe one of the most powerful things we can do in life is learn how to reflect—how to look into the rearview mirror of our lives—but when we look without the right posture, without the right mind and heart, we don't find clarity. We find condemnation.

What shows up in that mirror becomes a highlight reel of everything we've done wrong instead of the context we actually need to move forward.

Most people say they want to grow. They want clarity. They want to move forward with more confidence, more intention, and more peace than they had before. But what many people don't realize is that growth rarely begins with motivation or discipline. More often than not, it begins with reflection. And reflection, depending on how it is approached, can either become one of the most powerful tools for transformation or a subtle source of self-destruction.

Reflection itself is neutral. It doesn't carry meaning on its own. What gives it power—or strips it of its value—is the posture we bring into it. When reflection is rooted in shame, it becomes a rehearsal of regret. We replay conversations, decisions, and moments where things didn't go the way we hoped, not to learn from them, but to confirm an internal belief that something must be wrong with us. Over time, that kind of reflection doesn't lead to growth. It leads to hesitation, self-doubt, and eventually paralysis.

That's not what reflection was ever meant to do.

Reflection was never designed to be a courtroom where you put yourself on trial. It was meant to be a mirror that shows you the truth without distorting it. And the truth, when handled correctly, doesn't shame you into change. It invites you into it.

This is where the paradox begins to reveal itself. The same act of looking back can either imprison you or free you. Reflection driven by shame tends to ask questions that attack identity, questions like, "What's wrong with me?" or "Why do I always end up here?" Over time, those questions stop being questions and start becoming conclusions. Clarity-driven reflection, on the other hand, asks questions that lead somewhere. It asks, "What can I learn from this?" and "What is this season trying to show me?" The difference isn't subtle, and the outcomes couldn't be more different.

One posture closes you in on yourself. The other opens you up to growth.

Learning how to reflect without shame is one of the most important skills a person can develop. It allows you to look honestly at your life without turning against yourself in the process. It gives you the ability to acknowledge responsibility without assigning yourself a permanent label. It creates space between what happened and who you are, which is where healing and growth actually take place.

At the foundation of this kind of reflection is an understanding that awareness is not the enemy. Awareness is the doorway. Many people avoid reflection because they associate it with discomfort, but discomfort is often the signal that something meaningful is trying to surface. Avoidance doesn't remove patterns; it simply delays them. What goes unexamined doesn't disappear. It finds new ways to express itself, often in our reactions, our relationships, and our decisions.

This is why I often say that you cannot eliminate what you don't illuminate. The things we refuse to look at don't lose their influence over us. They gain it. Unprocessed emotions, unaddressed beliefs, and unresolved experiences tend to shape us quietly from the background, influencing how we show up long before we realize what's happening.

Many people work hard and still feel stuck because they are moving without awareness. They are doing more without seeing more. And movement without awareness often leads us back to the same place, just with more exhaustion attached to it. Reflection provides orientation. It helps you locate yourself honestly, without exaggeration or denial. It answers a question most people are hesitant to ask: where am I really?

Not where you wish you were. Not where others assume you are. But where you actually are.

That question requires courage, because the answer is rarely flattering. But it is always freeing. The challenge isn't that we've made mistakes. Everyone has. The challenge is the meaning we attach to those mistakes. Too often, we allow experiences to shape conclusions about our worth instead of seeing them as information about what needs to change. We move from observing behavior to questioning identity, and that shift is subtle, but it's dangerous.

Mistakes reveal behavior. They were never meant to define worth.

This distinction matters because without it, reflection becomes a weapon instead of a guide. With it, reflection becomes a tool that helps us move forward with humility, wisdom, and clarity rather than fear.

This distinction between behavior and identity is something I had to learn the hard way, and one of the most formative seasons where this lesson began to take root in my life came through my first divorce. During my junior year of college, my life shifted in a way I could never have anticipated. My father, Cornelius Royal Glasgow—still to this day one of the most influential men in my life—was diagnosed with a rare form of cancer called cholangiocarcinoma.

At the time, we were uneducated about it. We were ignorant to its severity and progression, and quite frankly, we thought it would simply become part of his story and testimony, something we would overcome together. But the disease progressed rapidly. In less than two years, my father lost over one hundred pounds. He went from being a strong, disciplined man to a frail figure who no longer had the ability to care for himself.

What began as something small, something we believed we could manage, became one of the most defining shifts in our family's life when we ultimately buried my father.

Even now, as I write this, I can still feel the weight of losing him. The uncertainty. The fear. The anger. The questions. The gratitude for the time we had. The grief of knowing there would be no more. I know there are stages of grief that we're told everyone goes through when they lose someone they love, but what isn't often talked about is that those stages don't move in a clean or predictable order. They don't give equal space. And for me, they never followed a script.

Even more than a decade later, the pain hasn't disappeared. It has simply lost its power to derail my day or pull me into the kind of depression it once did in the months following my father's death.

In the midst of that season, I met my first wife the mother of my daughter. We began building a relationship that, in reflection, was formed more out of pain than partnership. She became a companion in a moment when my world had been shaken, and she stood in the gap loving and caring for me when I didn't even know who I was or what I wanted for the future.

We were young—two kids trying to build a life together while navigating a world we didn't fully understand. We were finding security in each other as a way to address underlying trauma neither of us had the tools to process. And even though there was love, the relationship was built on brokenness rather than shared wholeness.

From that relationship came one of the greatest gifts of my life—my daughter. To this day, she is a reminder of how God can build the most beautiful things out of the most broken places.

Unfortunately, the relationship itself would come to an end in divorce, leaving both of us holding pieces of ourselves, trying to figure out how to rebuild our lives from what remained. For me, the concept of divorce was incredibly difficult to process. I came from parents who had been married for over two decades, moving toward three. I had no context for divorce growing up, and one of my deepest fears was ever allowing my daughter to live in something I had never experienced myself.

Yet there I was, facing a reality I hadn't planned for, carrying a story I didn't know how to integrate.

The narratives I began telling myself in that season were subtle but powerful. What I couldn't be. What I couldn't say. What I couldn't teach. How I couldn't help people moving forward. Before I ever discovered the purpose I'm walking in today, I felt disqualified to be a man of integrity and character because of what I perceived as a societal stain.

So when the door of purpose eventually opened in my life through a divine encounter, it was difficult for me to fully step into it. I carried the weight of my past mistakes into my present calling. I had the desire and the gifting to help others, but there was dissonance between who I was becoming and who I believed I had been.

That dissonance showed up as what I thought was imposter syndrome. But looking back now, I realize it was something deeper. It was identity sabotage. I was allowing my past to dictate my permission to show up fully in the present. I diluted my yes. I hesitated in my commitment to grow, to teach, to lead, to help others, because I believed the illusion that people who help others have their lives perfectly laid out.

We tend to associate impact with perfection, forgetting that most transformation comes from scars, not images. We compare ourselves to what we see on the surface while ignoring what's hidden beneath it—the challenges, the pain, the mistakes, the humanity that every single one of us carries.

I've come to believe that we don't fully step into impact until we're willing to embrace our journey honestly, not selectively. It wasn't until I made the decision to stop looking back through the lens of fear and start looking back through the lens of gratitude that everything began to change. I could finally acknowledge where I made mistakes without concluding that I was a mistake.

I wasn't broken beyond repair. I was a man navigating loss, uncertainty, and pain the best way I knew how at the time. And the only reason I know now that there was a better way is because I lived through it.

Today, as a performance advisor and coach, I help individuals and couples identify patterns that influence their lives and relationships. Even in my current marriage, with my beautiful wife, I'm able to show up with patience, love, and intentionality in ways that would not have been possible had I not embraced the truth about my history. That history only has the power to paralyze me if I look back believing I am what I've done, instead of recognizing that what I've done can give me context and clarity for how to move forward.

My mistakes can either imprison me or instruct me, depending on how I choose to reflect on them.

What I've learned through all of this is that your history only has the power you give it. It can either become a prison or a teacher. It can either paralyze you or prepare you. And the difference is not what happened to you, but how you choose to reflect on what happened to you.

This is why it's so important to understand that mistakes may come with consequences, but those consequences don't have to derail your life. They don't have to disqualify you from purpose. They don't have to define your future. They can become markers—scars that tell a story—not of failure, but of survival, resilience, and growth.

I am a firm believer that you can change the trajectory of your life by taking ownership of your story. Ownership doesn't mean self-blame. It means self-honesty. It means acknowledging what happened, recognizing your role in it, and deciding that it will not be the end of you. It means picking up the steering wheel of your history and intentionally pointing it in the direction of your destiny.

I have made mistakes, but I am not a mistake.
I have failed at some things, but I am not a failure.
I have disappointed people at times, but my life is not a disappointment.

Those distinctions matter, because without them, reflection becomes a place of punishment instead of progress.

I often ask people this question: what would your life look like if you reflected with gratitude instead of fear? If you looked back not to condemn yourself, but to understand yourself. If you reflected with the posture of learning instead of the posture of shame. Because shame will always keep you stuck in what was, while clarity gives you permission to move toward what can be.

To this day, I've never met a perfect person. And I know that if I ever do, I've probably just met someone who isn't being honest. Every person you admire has a story you don't fully know. Every life that looks aligned from the outside has required internal work that often goes unseen. The goal was never perfection. The goal has always been alignment.

When reflection turns into shame, it's usually a sign that we've crossed a line from accountability into self-condemnation. We stop saying, "That choice didn't serve me," and start saying, "There must be something wrong with me." Once that belief settles in, it begins to influence everything else. Shame doesn't motivate growth. It convinces you that growth is pointless.

Clarity, on the other hand, always leaves room for movement. It allows you to say, "This isn't who I am. This is where I am." And that distinction preserves identity while still inviting change.

Reflection without shame gives you the ability to observe your life with honesty and compassion at the same time. It creates space between what happened and who you are. It gives you room to breathe, to learn, and to adjust without losing your footing.

This kind of reflection also invites you to examine what you've normalized. Over time, many people quietly adapt to emotional exhaustion, misalignment, and disconnection simply because those states have become familiar. Familiarity can be deceptive. It can make unhealthy patterns feel acceptable and misalignment feel inevitable.

But normal does not always mean healthy.
And familiar does not always mean aligned.

Reflection without shame allows you to challenge those norms without attacking yourself. It invites curiosity instead of judgment. It asks questions like, "What am I tolerating that no longer serves me?"

and "What patterns have I accepted that conflict with the life I say I want to live?"

Growth requires that level of honesty. But it also requires compassion. You cannot grow in an environment where you are constantly under attack, even if that attack is coming from your own inner voice. Transformation requires safety. And safety begins with the way you speak to yourself when things don't go as planned.

This approach to reflection doesn't eliminate responsibility. It reframes it. It allows you to take ownership without destroying your confidence in the process. It keeps you connected to your worth while you confront what needs to shift.

As you move forward through this book, everything builds on this foundation. Awareness leads to ownership. Ownership strengthens identity. Identity informs alignment. Alignment shapes how you live. But none of it works if reflection becomes a weapon instead of a guide.

Reflection without shame is not avoidance. It is maturity. It is the ability to tell yourself the truth without abandoning yourself. And it is one of the most powerful practices you can develop if you want to live with intention, clarity, and peace.

This is the paradox of reflection. When you look back with fear, you stay stuck. When you look back with clarity, you move forward. The past doesn't lose its power because it's forgotten. It loses its power when it's understood.

And when reflection is done well, it doesn't trap you in who you were. It frees you to become who you're meant to be.

CHAPTER THREE

YOU CANNOT ELIMINATE WHAT YOU DON'T ILLUMINATE

HAVE YOU EVER found yourself going through the motions but not actually making movement? You're busy, you're active, you're doing all the "right" things—yet your life isn't reflecting the level of results, peace, or fulfillment you know you're capable of experiencing.

I'm talking about those seasons where you pause long enough to realize that your busyness and your effort are not equal to your breakthrough. You're checking boxes but not changing outcomes. You're expending energy, but you're not expanding impact.

I'm not a huge pet guy, but I'm always fascinated when I take my son—who loves animals—to the pet store. We'll walk slowly past the different tanks and cages, pointing out fish, birds, lizards. Eventually we get to the hamster section and, almost without fail, one little creature is sprinting on that wheel like its life depends on it. We'll stand there for a while, just watching this tiny athlete run in place for an extended period of time—burning a bunch of "pet calories," if that's even a thing—but not actually going anywhere.

What always strikes me is this: I wonder if the hamster realizes it's not actually moving. From the outside, it's obvious to everyone walking by that there's no real change in position for all of that effort. But from the hamster's perspective, the experience is different. It feels motion. It feels exertion. It feels speed. It feels like progress.

Many times, we find ourselves in that exact same position. Sometimes we finally realize our efforts are not materializing. Other times, we normalize this pattern of maximum effort with minimal movement to the point that we don't even recognize it until someone who loves us—or someone responsible for developing us—holds up a mirror and says, "Hey, do you realize you're literally running on the hamster wheel of life?"

It looks like this: you're working, achieving, serving, doing all the things you believe you're supposed to do—yet you carry this quiet, persistent desire to see something different happen. You're exhausted, but not fulfilled. Busy, but not aligned. You're showing up for everyone and everything, but deep down you know you're not really showing up for yourself. No matter how much effort you put in, it feels like you're living in a cycle.

I firmly believe this way of living eventually produces frustration that, if left unchecked, can lead to numbness, bitterness, and even depression. This isn't a small thing that can be casually ignored. It's not just "a busy season." It is a pattern we have to confront and disrupt, because the alternative is to spend our lives existing instead of actually living.

There is a thin line between existing and living. Existing is when you wake up, go through your routines, hit your obligations, and collapse into bed knowing you survived another day—but with no sense that you truly inhabited it. Living is when you step into your days with intention, with alignment, with a sense that your energy is being invested, not just spent.

Life is meant to be lived. In order to move away from just surviving and step into thriving, we have to confront this hamsterwheel life and eradicate our acceptance of it by any means necessary.

This chapter is about exactly that. It's an invitation to stop confusing motion with progress and to start illuminating the undercurrents that keep you spinning in place. Because you cannot eliminate what you refuse to illuminate.

THREE WAYS THE HAMSTER WHEEL SHOWS UP

Whenever we face the reality of the hamsterwheel life, we usually discover there are a few different ways it shows up. On the surface, it just feels like "I'm stuck." But underneath that feeling, there are at least three distinct patterns:

1. We're not making progress because we're doing the wrong thing.
2. We're pursuing the right thing at the wrong time.
3. We want the right thing at the right time, but we're carrying the wrong thought life.

Let's break each one down as we lay the foundation for what it's going to look like to do the deep, honest work that leads to real transformation.

THE WRONG THING: CHASING WHAT WAS NEVER YOURS

First, let's talk about the wrong thing and the journey of becoming.

It has never been easier to chase something that was never designed for you. We are swimming in a culture that is driven by the external at the cost of the internal. Every scroll offers you a highlight reel of somebody else's life, body, relationship, platform, or success.

It's easy to lock onto something that looks good on someone else without ever asking if it was actually meant for you.

We start going after outcomes—titles, lifestyles, income levels, even versions of success—without ever pausing long enough to ask ourselves a simple but confronting question:

Is the thing I'm going after really for me, or did I just assume it would look good on me because I saw it look good on someone else?

In my first book, *Take Back Your Power,* I wrote, "What you chase will always run from you, but what you pursue will find you." My argument is that many of us live our entire lives chasing things because we've seen them look good on someone else, while spending very little time pursuing what is truly ours.

The problem with chasing what looks good on others is that you never actually catch it. Here's how it plays out:

- You chase a dream home because it looked perfect for your neighbor. You finally build your version of it…only to see an even bigger, "better" house going up next door.
- You chase the kind of partner you see someone else with and, in the process, diminish the partner you chose. Eventually you realize every relationship comes with flaws, tension, and growth areas—and the grass isn't always greener on the other side. It just looks that way from a distance. I like to say, "The grass does look greener on the other side—until you get the water bill."

Constantly, we spend our lives chasing what we've seen instead of pursuing what we know, deep in our spirit, to be ours.

This hamsterwheel of chasing the wrong thing has actually been one of the hidden blessings of my life. I spent years pursuing opportunities, partnerships, and clients I was convinced were perfect for me. I couldn't understand why the door of opportunity kept closing in my face.

Fastforward a few years, and clarity set in. I realized one client I had been chasing was on the edge of catastrophe. One partnership I desperately wanted involved someone tied up in crime and lacking integrity. A platform I thought I needed came with such a messy reputation that standing on that stage would have derailed me before my career even got started.

At the time, every "no" felt like rejection. Looking back, those closed doors were protection.

The hamster wheel of chasing the wrong thing often turns into a blessing—but only after we realize it was the wrong thing. While we're in the chase, though, before we see it clearly, the experience is often frustration and anger, because what we think we want feels equal to what we believe we really need. Losing it feels like life is withholding oxygen.

Maybe you're in that space right now. You're doing everything you know to do. You're chasing what you were told is "success." But your soul is tired, your peace is thin, and your joy feels conditional. If that's you, you may not be lazy, unmotivated, or behind. You may simply be pouring everything you have into something that was never meant to be yours.

THE WRONG TIME: WANTING IT BEFORE IT'S READY

The second hamster wheel is wanting the right thing at the wrong time.

I struggled to write this part, because timing has been the kryptonite of my journey. If you know me, you'd probably consider me not just Type A, but Type A+. My ambition has always been one of my greatest strengths. I've often said that while most people are still talking about an idea, I'm already ten miles down the road building what I see.

This drive is celebrated in our culture. We applaud people who selfinitiate, who create, who move fast, who refuse to wait for permission. That level of ambition comes with real rewards: doors open, opportunities appear, momentum builds.

But there's a cost. The duality of ambition is that the same drive that accelerates your progress can also accelerate your pain. It can cost you relationships, health, and peace in ways that cannot be fully captured in words.

I believe one of my Godgiven gifts is the gift of foresight or vision—the ability to see, in business, in strategy, in people, what they can become. I often see the solution before most people have fully named the problem. That's a gift. But here's what I've had to learn the hard way:

Vision and ambition without patience is a recipe for disaster.

Seeing it doesn't necessarily mean it's time to seize it. Just because you can see the future version of a thing—a business, a relationship, a platform, a ministry—doesn't mean that version exists yet. And when you try to live in a version that has not yet matured, you end up placing expectations on yourself and others that nobody is prepared to carry.

So I found myself in seasons of deep frustration because I wanted the right thing…but I wanted it now.

This hamster wheel feels different from chasing the wrong thing. The hamster wheel of "right thing, wrong time" doesn't just burn emotional energy; it burns through resources, relationships, and moments that should be sacred. You rush past dinners, milestones, and conversations, aggressively trying to accelerate the process toward the promise. You're convinced that if you move fast enough, push hard enough, sacrifice enough, you can make the future arrive on your schedule.

In those seasons, you may be ready—but the thing is not ready. The world around it is not ready. The people connected to it are not ready. The infrastructure required to sustain it is not ready.

Ultimately, if you're living on assignment, timing is part of your calling. What you're responsible to bring into this world is not just about what you do, but when you do it. Some doors are only healthy to walk through at a particular stage of your development. Some opportunities are only safe once your character has caught up with your charisma.

If that resonates with you, this chapter isn't about shaming your ambition. It's about aligning your pace with your purpose so you're not perpetually exhausted from outrunning your own assignment.

THE WRONG THOUGHT LIFE: ABLE TO ATTAIN, UNABLE TO SUSTAIN

The third hamster wheel is the wrong thought life.

Here's where many of us get blindsided: we want the right thing, at the right time, but we approach it with a thought life that cannot sustain it. We think success is mostly about showing up, doing the work, and "getting the thing." We forget that life has a way of exposing whatever we haven't dealt with internally.

I've always said, "Getting the thing is easy; managing it is exposing."

What I mean is this: you can go after something and even obtain it. You can get the promotion, launch the business, publish the book, marry the person, step into the role. But if you don't understand that getting the thing is one assignment and managing the magnitude of what comes with it is another, you will struggle.

The hamster wheel of "able to attain but unable to sustain" shows up like this:

- Opportunities arrive, but you fumble them because your selfworth says, "I don't deserve this."
- Doors open, but your fear of being truly seen causes you to sabotage them.
- You achieve something meaningful, but your thought life refuses to let you enjoy it. You're already worrying about losing it, being criticized for it, or being exposed as "not enough."

This hamster wheel doesn't just waste opportunities; it wears down your confidence. After dropping enough balls, you start to believe the lie that you're inconsistent, unqualified, or cursed—when in reality, you may simply be unprepared in your inner world for what you've been praying for in your outer world.

Understanding these three hamster wheels—the wrong thing, the wrong time, and the wrong thought life—is just the beginning. Seeing where they show up in your life is important. But going deeper—beyond the hamster wheel and into what we'll call in this chapter the patterns and undercurrents—is where transformation really begins.

WAVES AND WIND: PATTERNS AND UNDERCURRENTS

One of the most important lessons in my own journey has been learning to discern the undercurrents of my life. Many of us are fighting battles and losing them because we're fighting the wave instead of the wind.

The wave is what you can see. The wind is what you can't.
Patterns are the waves. Undercurrents are the wind.

Think about the ocean. Standing on the shore, you see waves rising and crashing. But those waves aren't random. They're created by wind—force you cannot see, blowing across the surface of the water, forming ripples that, over time, become waves. The stronger and more consistent the wind, the greater the wave.

In the same way, the visible problems in your life—the arguments, the burnout cycles, the procrastination, the financial chaos, the broken relationships—are waves. They're real. They're disruptive. They demand attention. But they are not root causes. They're the result of winds that have been blowing beneath the surface for a long time.

The truth is simple but not always easy to live:

You cannot eliminate what you don't illuminate.

This chapter is an invitation to move past the surface level of your life and dive into the undercurrents that are shaping your progress, your peace, your fulfillment, and your sense of direction. Many people are stuck not because they lack skill, education, or opportunity, but because they haven't yet found the courage to confront what has been quietly chasing them for years.

You cannot reach the level of confidence and freedom you desire without first reaching clarity. And clarity only comes when you're willing to confront the source of the issue, not just the symptoms it produces.

In Chapter One, we talked about not quitting on yourself. In Chapter Two, we explored reflection without shame. This chapter is where those two ideas meet: you choose to stay with yourself while you shine a light on what needs to change.

To do that, we're going to look at two key ideas:

1. Patterns: the waves you keep meeting.
2. Undercurrents: the wind beneath those waves.

PATTERNS: THE WAVES YOU KEEP MEETING

Patterns are the experiences, behaviors, and outcomes that keep repeating in your life—even when the people, places, and circumstances change. They're the cycles that don't lead to progress but to paralysis and stagnation.

Patterns sound like this:

- The same argument shows up in every relationship, even with completely different people.
- Your money story never changes: the moment you get ahead, something "always" happens.

- You hit the same burnout cycle every year, no matter what job, city, or church you're in.
- You find yourself consistently undervalued at work or overlooked for opportunities, regardless of the organization.

Patterns are dangerous partly because of how quietly they normalize themselves. Over time, we stop questioning them. We start saying things like, "This is just how my life is," or "This is just the way I am." Financial chaos, constant drama, cycles of overwork, chronic selfdoubt—these experiences become familiar. And familiarity has a way of numbing us to the possibility that what we're living with is not what we were created for.

In the next chapter, *When Normal Isn't Healthy*, we're going to dive deep into how harmful patterns disguise themselves as "normal." For now, I want you to remember one thing:

Patterns are not destiny. *They are signals.*

They are evidence that something beneath the surface hasn't been addressed. They are the waves that tell you there's wind blowing somewhere in your life that needs your attention.

In my own life, one of the clearest patterns showed up while I was building my team.

I've been on this journey of entrepreneurship and impact for years now—traveling to major cities, speaking on big stages, consulting with organizations. From the outside, it looked like momentum. But underneath it all, there was a repeating feeling: loneliness.

I spent countless hours alone—studying, preparing, traveling—so that for an hour on stage, I could show up with excellence. Deep down, I believed that if I could just build the right ATeam, the loneliness would go away.

So I started partnering with people. But if I'm honest, my decisions weren't always logical; they were emotional. I wasn't just looking for collaborators. I was looking for people to heal. I was drawn to highcapacity individuals whose potential had been mishandled by life. I felt a responsibility to help them become who I believed they could be—sometimes even when they hadn't asked for that.

Part of that is connected to my calling. I am called to develop leaders, to help people tap into their potential. But here's where it got complicated: I had to learn that the team serving with me cannot become the mission I'm called to accomplish. If they do, then instead of going together to serve others, those serving with me become spectators on the sideline of a game they're also called to play.

So much of our ability to do the work we're called to do at the highest level is connected to the support we have around us. But when that support becomes a need we have to fulfill—when every team member becomes a project we must rescue—our essence gets split. Our focus fractures. And that lack of focus eventually affects our effectiveness.

I'm not saying that as leaders we shouldn't pour into people. What I recognized is that there is a fine line between working together to accomplish a mission and one of us becoming the mission. When that line is crossed, focus is divided and impact is diluted.

On the surface, the wave looked like this: disappointment. Yet another person who "didn't want it as badly" as I did. Yet another failed partnership. Yet another team member who seemed to fade out.

But when I finally paid attention to the pattern—after repeating it more than once—I saw the wind.

I was trying to build my belief in my own value by how much I could change the people closest to me. I questioned my authenticity because I could move organizations but felt stuck with my own team. What looked like a team problem was—at its core—an identity problem. I didn't fully believe in me, so I tried to prove my worth by fixing others.

That's the danger of ignoring undercurrents. You can want the right thing—healthy teams, strong relationships, meaningful impact—

but if you want it from the wrong place, it will never fully be the right thing.

THE UNDERCURRENT: WIND BENEATH THE WAVE

Growing up in the Caribbean, I was surrounded by beaches. Our waves weren't massive like some places in the world, but I learned early that waves don't appear out of nowhere. They are created by wind.

Wind blows across the surface of the water, forming ripples. As the wind grows stronger and more consistent, those ripples become waves. The greater the wind, the greater the wave.

That windandwave dynamic is one of the clearest ways to understand how patterns operate in your life.

Most of us spend our energy trying to manage the wave—the visible crisis, the argument, the late bill, the missed deadline, the toxic dynamic at work—without spending nearly as much time asking what kind of wind has been blowing beneath the surface.

> The wave says, "I keep choosing the wrong relationships."
> The wind says, "Somewhere deep down, I don't believe I deserve better."

> The wave says, "I always procrastinate."
> The wind says, "If I never start, I never have to face the fear of failing."

> The wave says, "I'm always overcommitted."
> The wind says, "I'm more afraid of disappointing people than I am of disappointing myself."

Identifying the wave matters. It's the pattern that alerts you something isn't right. But if you stop there, the pattern will simply find a new way to show up. You can switch jobs, cities, churches, or circles, and the same dynamics will eventually reappear—because the wind never changed.

You could say it like this: if you don't notice the fruit, you'll never suspect there's a rotten root. But if you never do the root work, that fruit keeps growing back.

Root work takes humility. It takes courage. It requires a willingness to sit with uncomfortable truths and ask questions you may have avoided for years. For some people, that work begins in an honest conversation or a moment of quiet reflection. For others, it unfolds over months of coaching, counseling, or intentional journaling. For too many, it never happens at all—because they never slow down long enough to look beneath the surface.

FOUR UNDERCURRENTS THAT SHAPE YOUR LIFE

Let's name some of the most common winds—the undercurrents that drive our patterns.

1. LIMITING BELIEFS

We'll go deep on limiting beliefs in the next chapter, but for now, think of them as stories you've accepted as true. They sound like:

- "People like me don't get opportunities like that."
- "If I let people see the real me, they'll leave."
- "I'm good at starting things, but I never follow through."

These beliefs become lenses. You don't just have them; you look through them. They filter your conversations, your risks, your disappointments, and even your compliments. A simple piece of feedback becomes confirmation that you're not enough. A door opening feels like a fluke instead of favor.

For now, it's enough to notice that behind many of your patterns is a belief you've never really examined—a story you've lived inside without realizing you had a choice.

2. INHERITED NARRATIVES

Inherited narratives are the stories you didn't consciously choose but absorbed from family, culture, environment, or early experiences. Nobody had to sit you down and spell them out; you learned them from tone, facial expressions, reactions, and unspoken rules.

They sound like:

- "Don't dream too big; people like us need to be realistic."
- "Keep your head down. Don't make waves."
- "We don't talk about that."

One of the strongest inherited narratives in my life was about acceptance. I developed an insatiable appetite for excellence—one that produced extraordinary results but often at the cost of my peace.

Growing up in a small Caribbean nation and then getting the chance to come to the United States, there was this unspoken pressure: Now you have to become something. I still remember not scoring high enough on my exams to attend one of the top high schools back home. My father, an educator, was disappointed. As his son, I felt like I hadn't just failed a test; I had failed him.

Those early moments quietly linked love and acceptance with performance in my mind. If I did well, I was worthy. If I fell short, I was a disappointment.

Years later, I could see how that wind was still blowing. So much of my drive was rooted in a desire to be accepted. Excellence itself isn't the problem; it's beautiful. But when excellence becomes the only way you believe you can be loved, it births waves of burnout, overcommitment, and chronic selfcriticism.

3. UNPROCESSED PAIN

Unprocessed pain is the hurt you never fully acknowledged, grieved, or healed. It doesn't disappear; it disguises itself. It shows up as:

- defensiveness when someone offers feedback
- detachment when relationships get too close
- perfectionism that makes it impossible to rest

Pain that isn't processed gets repurposed. It leaks into your decisions, your tone, your boundaries. Often, what looks like "just how I am" is actually "who I became to survive what happened."

My own deeper dive into this work was accelerated by a coffin.

When my father died of cancer, I remember seeing him in the casket and feeling like the man who had been Superman to me suddenly became mortal. I leaned over, kissed his cold cheek, and in that moment something in me made a vow: I've got you. I'll finish what you started.

From that day, the clock started. I ran hard toward purpose and calling. A mentor once described me as one of the most driven people he had ever met, and for a long time I wore that as a badge of honor. The results seemed to justify it—doors opened, stages expanded, testimonies poured in.

From the outside, it looked like pure passion. But the undercurrent was different. I wasn't just driven to something; I was driven from something.

I was running from the fear of reaching my own coffin one day with unfulfilled potential. That kind of fear makes you rush the process, lose patience with people, and sometimes break what's around you so you don't miss what's in you. I could stand on stages and proclaim, "Your pain can be the catalyst for your purpose," and I still believe that. But now I add this:

Until you address that pain, you will never have peace. And there is no such thing as walking in true purpose without peace.

4. "NORMAL" THAT ISN'T HEALTHY

Over time, we normalize things that are quietly draining us:

- working at a pace that requires constant burnout and recovery
- staying in relationships where our worth is constantly questioned
- living with relentless inner criticism and calling it "standards"

There was a season where my schedule, my stress level, and my selftalk had all become "normal" to me. I treated exhaustion as a badge of honor and constant availability as proof of my commitment. Looking back, I can see it wasn't noble—it was numbing.

We'll explore this more in *When Normal Isn't Healthy*, but for now remember: normal is not the same as healthy, and familiarity is not the same as alignment.

ILLUMINATING WITHOUT ATTACKING YOURSELF

If we stopped here, this could feel heavy. That's not the goal. Illumination is not about selfattack. It's about selfhonesty.

In the previous chapter, we talked about reflection without shame—learning to look back not to condemn yourself but to understand yourself. That same posture is what allows you to illuminate these undercurrents without turning on yourself in the process.

This work is not about labeling yourself as broken, unworthy, or beyond repair. It's about telling the truth so you can participate in your own healing.

Here are some simple questions to begin the work of illumination:

- **Pattern**: What keeps repeating in my life, even when the people and places change?

- **Belief**: What must I be believing for this pattern to make sense?
- **Origin**: Where did I learn that? Who did I watch model that?
- **Truth**: Is this actually true, or did it just feel true for a long time?
- **Alignment**: What would I choose if I believed something different?

You don't have to answer all of these in one sitting. This isn't a test; it's a conversation with yourself. The goal is not to fix everything overnight, but to start turning the light on in rooms you've kept dim for years.

Many people work hard and still feel stuck because they're moving without awareness. They're doing more without seeing more. And movement without awareness usually leads back to the same place—just with more exhaustion.

Illumination doesn't magically solve everything, but it changes the game. Once you see a pattern, you can't unsee it. Once you can say, "This isn't just happening to me; I'm participating in it," you reclaim power. The light may sting at first, especially if you've spent years in the dark. But over time, that same light becomes your guide.

FROM AUTOPILOT TO ALIGNMENT

Not quitting on you (Chapter One) requires this kind of honesty. Reflection without shame (Chapter Two) prepares you to face truth. This chapter is where those two meet: you choose to stay with yourself while you look at what needs to change.

As you continue this journey, you'll start to notice a powerful theme: the things you once called "just who I am" may actually be who you became in response to what happened. That realization can feel disorienting, but it's also deeply hopeful. If you learned it, you can unlearn it. If you accepted it, you can decline it. If you normalized it, you can redefine it.

Before you move on, I want to invite you into one simple practice.

Choose one area of your life where you feel stuck right now—relationships, work, finances, health, faith, or identity. Take ten minutes and walk through the five questions:

- Pattern
- Belief
- Origin
- Truth
- Alignment

Don't overthink it. Don't edit yourself. Just write. Let the light in.

You are not stuck because you're broken. You're stuck because you've been fighting the wave while the wind kept blowing.

And you cannot eliminate what you're still unwilling to illuminate.

In the next chapter, we're going to zoom in on one of the most powerful undercurrents of all: your beliefs—the stories you've been telling yourself about who you are, what you deserve, what's possible for you, and how life works. Once we begin to illuminate those beliefs, you'll see just how much of your life has been shaped not by your potential, but by your perception.

CHAPTER FOUR

BREAK FREE FROM LIMITING BELIEFS

As I sit down to write this chapter on limiting beliefs, I feel it's important to remove the cape and speak from a place most wouldn't expect—vulnerable, unfiltered, and honest.

Whether you've seen me deliver a keynote, watched me teach a masterclass, or been coached by me oneonone, you've likely experienced the energy, power, confidence, and faith I bring into every space. But what you see in public is not always the full story. The moments of inspiration you witness are often built in the shadows of my own internal wrestling—when there's no stage, no spotlight, no audience.

It's in the quiet—in my office, scrolling through Instagram without intention, lying on the couch watching Netflix—that I've battled the invisible enemy of inadequacy. I fight feelings that question my value, my gift, my contribution. And what's wild is that these feelings can creep in even after the most powerful moments. I can come off stage after receiving a standing ovation and still question, midflight on the way home, whether what I shared was enough. Did I really make an impact? Was it truly significant?

These thoughts have a way of becoming loud in the spaces between—the gaps between sessions, stages, and wins. Over time I've come to understand that while others may see the glory, that glory was built through grit in the garage of growth. The real battle I face is not external. It's the inner war between the king in me—and the boy still fighting to believe he belongs.

When I refer to myself as a king, it's not from a place of arrogance, but of birthright. A king leads. A king builds. A king stewards. A king creates space for others to rise. But even kings can feel like imposters—especially when the boy inside them is still bleeding.

That boy inside me? He's why I still have wonder. He's the reason I dream with reckless hope. He's the heartbeat of my curiosity, the spark that keeps me trying. But he also carries scars. Wounds formed during years of childhood ridicule.

I grew up on an island full of beauty—white sand, blue skies, vibrant culture. But that beauty didn't protect me from pain. Especially in high school, I was bullied. Bullied in ways no kid should have to endure.

If you've ever been bullied, you already know—kids can be cruel. And while I'd always loved school growing up, something shifted when I transitioned from the innocent joy of childhood into a high school culture that fed off judgment, ridicule, and shame.

For me, it started with my head. Literally.

Kids laughed at me for having a larger head than most. It was a trait I never thought twice about until it became a target. That ridicule had a lasting effect. I began shrinking in rooms I was meant to stand in. I avoided conversations. I stayed quiet in class. I sat alone in cafeterias. I disappeared in the spaces I once loved.

Even now, as a grown man, it's hard to admit how deeply that ridicule affected me. I laugh about it today, but back then, I only laughed to survive—not because I was okay.

We don't often realize there's something "wrong" with us until someone convinces us that there is.

That's what bullying does. It plants doubt in places that once felt secure. It creates narratives that shape how we see ourselves. It doesn't just bruise our egos—it rewrites our identities.

I remember finally breaking down in front of my father, tears in my eyes, sharing the torment I was experiencing. His response was simple: "Boy, man up."

So I did.

I straightened my back. Dried my tears. But what I didn't know then was that I wasn't truly "manning up"—I was burying. I was suppressing. And I was misunderstanding what true manhood even was.

His response, though wellintentioned, left another scar. It taught me that pain had no place. That emotion was weakness. That silence was strength. But real strength, I've learned, is in ownership, not avoidance. In facing the wounds, not hiding them.

That moment didn't make me tougher. It made me more determined to hide. It built a shell around my spirit. And inside that shell, I developed a desperate hunger for one thing: validation.

I just wanted to be accepted. To be enough. To matter.

That hunger followed me into adulthood. It showed up in my relationships, my work, and even my pursuit of impact. I began performing more than I was being. Pleasing more than I was leading. Seeking approval from people who never had the power to define me in the first place.

Here's what I've come to realize:

The need for validation is the kryptonite of vision.

Vision is internal, Godgiven, and anchored in truth. Validation is external, often fickle, and rooted in perception. When you let the outside dictate what's happening inside, you dilute your own power.

And where did all of this stem from? A limiting belief.

We don't just carry limiting beliefs—we create them.

We create them to cope with inadequacy.

A limiting belief, in its most profound sense, is an *inaccurate interpretation of our essence that results in selfsabotaging tendencies*. It's a false narrative that convinces you to play small, show up late, or not show up at all.

The bullying didn't just hurt—it shaped the story I told myself about myself. That story became a pattern. That pattern became a belief. That belief became a wall between who I was and who I was called to be.

And I'm not alone in this.

I've coached people twice my age who are still shackled by childhood wounds—divorce, instability, poverty, abuse, abandonment, even unprocessed privilege. Experiences that, when left unhealed, create gaps in selfworth. To fill those gaps, we build beliefs—beliefs that limit us from being all that we are.

But what if the thing you've been hiding, shrinking, or questioning…is actually your greatest source of power?

What if your weakness is your weapon—mismanaged?

Here's what I believe:

Limiting beliefs are not just lies—they're indicators.

They point to the exact place where your power lives.

What I was bullied for—the size of my head—is now symbolic. I don't run from it anymore. It houses my mind. My thoughts. My vision. My voice. And what they tried to ridicule…God has redeemed.

So here's what we're going to do in this chapter:

- We're going to identify the types of limiting beliefs that hold us back.
- We're going to trace them to their roots.
- We're going to uncover the inadequacy beneath them.
- And we're going to reclaim what was never lost—only forgotten.

It's time to stop playing small.

It's time to silence the lies.

It's time to break free from limiting beliefs.

You in?

THREE MASKS OF LIMITING BELIEFS

Limiting beliefs rarely walk in the front door announcing themselves. They show up wearing masks. In this chapter, we're going to pull back three of the most common:

1. Insecurity
2. Imposter Syndrome
3. Inflation of Self (Ego)

As you read, pay attention to where you see yourself. You may recognize one mask, or you may realize you've worn all three at different times.

Insecurities: *Thoughts Rooted in Doubt About Your Value*

I've had countless conversations with individuals from all walks of life—different backgrounds, cultures, and stages—and I've come to realize this: limiting beliefs show up in many disguises. One of the most subtle, yet powerful, is insecurity.

Let me be clear from the start: *insecurity is often a repetition of someone else's broken perspective that we have allowed to become our reality.*

It's easy to assume that this broken perspective always comes from someone else—a parent, a boss, an ex, a peer. But many times, the repetition comes from our own internal dialogue. We become the narrator of our own limitations.

I've heard people casually say things like, "I'm not good enough," "I'm so stupid," or "I always mess things up." They say these things to express a moment of frustration, but those words are seeds—seeds that, when repeated, grow roots in the subconscious and begin to poison the soil of our identity.

Insecurity rarely starts loud. It often enters quietly, like a whisper in the back of your mind. But over time, the whisper becomes a theme, and that theme becomes the soundtrack of your life.

I tell people often: your words have power. That's not some motivational mantra. It's neurological and spiritual truth. Words leave your mouth and enter your ears. When you speak something often enough, your subconscious begins to believe it. Mouth to ear becomes a feedback loop feeding your mind. And your mind, when fed consistently, becomes the architect of your actions.

Try this with me: say out loud, "I'm not good enough." Now repeat it two more times. Then pause and notice the atmosphere shift inside you—the heaviness, the weight, the subtle sadness.

Now, breathe deeply. Say instead, "I am strong. I am bold. I am courageous." Say it again. And again. Do you feel that? The lift? The difference?

Words change atmospheres.

Our words are the auditory expression of our focus. And whatever you focus on grows. If you magnify negativity, it expands. If you magnify truth, possibility, and worth—you maximize those, too.

These insecurities, whether birthed through the words of a parent, an ex, a bully, or even yourself, live because we keep feeding them—through repetition, through agreement, through silence.

That's why I'm cautious with what I say about myself—even in jest. I won't joke about drinking poison, so I won't speak poison over my identity. I treat words with reverence because I've seen their power. Words can create wounds—but words can also heal them.

When I lost my father, I didn't initially seek therapy. But I began speaking life—to others and to myself. I truly believe my healing began the moment I became a vessel of healing for others. The residue of the words I spoke to lift others ended up healing the cracks in my own heart. What we give often comes back.

Here's the truth: your insecurities don't live on their own. They survive because you've created an environment for them—an environment of agreement. When you stop agreeing with them—through your words, your associations, your focus—they begin to die. They diminish wherever worth is established.

Worth can be established through the words you speak, but also through the books you read, the environments you choose, the people you surround yourself with, the habits you embrace, the vision you pursue.

The limiting belief of insecurity causes us to disqualify ourselves from moments we were born for. Whatever we struggle with, we assume others can see. We project our doubts onto their faces.

When I coach communicators in my *Speak with Conviction* program, I teach them not to judge the audience by their facial expressions. You can't know what they're thinking. Some of the people who look the least interested are the ones being most impacted. But your insecurity will trick you into filling the silence with a story—and that story usually mirrors your deepest fears.

What if those thoughts you've been believing are actually wrong? What if you've disqualified yourself from rooms you were built to dominate simply because of an insecurity?

On the other side of insecurity is not arrogance—it's authenticity. It's the ability to stand in who you are without apology. It's the capacity to carry your gift without needing validation. It's the presence that says, "I'm not perfect, but I'm powerful."

Some of my most impactful moments have come when I shared my gift without overthinking, without overanalyzing, without obsessing over how it would be received. When I simply showed up and let the gift speak for itself.

You don't need to prove your worth. You need to stop poisoning it.

Simple Practice:
Write down three phrases you often say about yourself when you're frustrated. Then, next to each one, write a truthfilled statement that honors who you really are. Read those truths out loud every day this week.

Don't let the power of your presence be drowned in the noise of your own insecurity. Your legacy is too important for that.

Imposter Syndrome: *The Illusion of Inadequacy Dressed as Perfection*

As we continue dismantling the limiting beliefs that attempt to rob you of your destiny and legacy, it's only right we address insecurity's twin sibling: imposter syndrome.

Imposter syndrome is the fear of being exposed as less than people think you are—even when the evidence says you're capable.

I'll be honest—I hadn't even heard the term "imposter syndrome" until I moved to the United States. I was in a coaching session when a client said, "That's something I really struggle with." It caught me off guard, so I started asking questions. What I uncovered was profound.

When I think of an imposter, I think of someone inserting themselves into a space where they weren't invited. We've all seen it—that person who shows up uninvited to a conversation or a room and forces their way in. Beneath that behavior is usually a deeper need—a fear of being left out. The act of imposing isn't the root; it's the response. It's a mask worn to avoid the pain of exclusion.

Imposter syndrome, at its core, is that same fear turned inward. It's the fear of being found out. The fear you're not as capable, prepared, or deserving as people think. It's not just insecurity; it's a sabotaging of opportunity rooted in the lie that readiness must look like perfection.

We've convinced ourselves that unless we meet an imagined standard of flawlessness, we're disqualified. So we hide. We hesitate. We shrink. We forfeit what's rightfully ours.

Most people struggling with imposter syndrome are not inadequate—they're comparing their process to someone else's pinnacle. And when comparison becomes the metric, perfection becomes the prison.

I've wrestled with this.

When I first stepped into speaking, I told myself:

- My accent will be a barrier.
- My voice doesn't carry enough authority.
- I don't have enough stories or humor to connect.
- My life isn't all the way together—who am I to help others?

All of those thoughts were rooted in comparison. I grew up hearing giants like Dr. Myles Munroe, Les Brown, Zig Ziglar. I judged my beginnings against their mastery. I confused their polish with their starting point and convinced myself I wasn't ready.

We do this so often—comparing our rough draft to someone else's published book, our behindthescenes to their highlight reel.

The need to be perfect—the version of ourselves we believe we must become before we start—is what keeps us from ever beginning.

Let's call it what it is:

Perfection is procrastination in disguise.

Perfection says, "If it's not flawless, it's not ready."

Imposter syndrome convinces us that the only way to show up is fully polished and fully prepared. But growth doesn't happen in arrival. It happens in movement. You don't become great by waiting—you become great by working.

When we're afraid to fail publicly, we avoid the very stages, rooms, and opportunities that were built to refine us. We believe exposure is dangerous—but what if exposure is divine? What if being in over your head is proof you're growing?

Vusi Thembekwayo, a brilliant business mind, once shared that he uses imposter syndrome as fuel. Not feeling polished enough? Prepare more. Not feeling confident enough? Study more. Not feeling ready? Practice harder. That shift—from insecurity to improvement—is a gamechanger.

Imposter syndrome doesn't have to be your anchor. It can be your engine. But only if you decide to stop waiting for perfection and start pursuing progress.

Let me remind you:

You are not an imposter.
You are becoming.

You're not underqualified—you're under process.
And just because you feel fear doesn't mean you lack faith.

Simple Practice:
Write down one area where you feel like a fraud. Underneath it, list three "receipts"—specific moments where you showed up and it went well. Let the evidence speak louder than the emotion.

On the other side of that doubt is the next level of your purpose. Don't let the lie of inadequacy rob you of it. Giving only half of yourself to avoid risk will only ever produce a fraction of what you're capable of.

So show up. Fully. Boldly. Authentically.

Not because you're perfect.

But because you're in purpose.

Inflation of Self (Ego): *The Mask That Looks Like Strength but Is Built on Fear*

I hope by now the scales are falling off your eyes, the weight is lifting off your shoulders, and the cage around your heart is cracking open. Because this journey isn't just about awareness—it's about liberation.

As we enter this third mask of limiting belief, I tread carefully. Not because it lacks truth, but because it's one of the easiest to see in others—and the hardest to recognize in ourselves. This next mask is ego.

We often think of ego as arrogance—a puffedup presence. The person who always has to be the loudest, the smartest, the best dressed, the most praised. It's easy to point fingers and place that image on someone else.

But here's the truth:

We are great lawyers for our own flaws and great judges of others' failures.

If we're not careful, each of us can struggle with ego—what I call an inflation of self. It often wears the costume of confidence. It can even be mistaken for charisma. But unlike confidence, which is rooted in truth, alignment, and clarity, ego is rooted in fear. It's a survival mechanism we construct when we feel threatened by our own shortcomings.

We all desire confidence. We want to walk into rooms with boldness. We want to own our space and our story. Confidence is necessary—but when it's built on how we look rather than who we are, it becomes ego.

There's a constant tension in our culture between looking good and being good.

Looking good seeks validation.
Being good seeks alignment.
Looking good is performative.
 Being good is purposeful.

Ego thrives in the first. True confidence lives in the second.

Ego is born the moment our identity becomes more about how others perceive us than who we truly are. It whispers, "You must appear perfect, or you'll be rejected." So we inflate ourselves—our accomplishments, our persona, our presence—as a defense.

But here's the irony:

Ego doesn't protect you. *It isolates you.*

It cuts you off from the very things that help you grow—like account-ability. Ego views accountability as an attack instead of an anchor. It resists correction, avoids feedback, and assumes any challenge to its perspective is a threat.

Life without accountability is a life headed toward destruction.

Why? Because accountability is the guardrail that keeps your purpose from crashing.

The inflated self also resists growth. It treats new information like an insult. It clings to outdated strategies. It stays stuck in patterns that feel comfortable but keep you stagnant. It's so committed to looking right that it never becomes better.

And perhaps most damaging of all, ego competes. It compares. It tears others down to feel taller. It defines success by being ahead of everyone else, not by being in alignment with purpose.

Let me be clear:

This is one of the most deceptive limiting beliefs because it can look like drive. It can even look like leadership. But it's actually fueled by the fear that you are not enough unless you're more than everyone else.

The inflation of self will always—always—lead to isolation. And when you live in isolation long enough, you start to believe the echo of your own voice is truth. You begin to think, "I don't need anyone. I can do it all myself." But eventually, ego turns on you.

Because one day life will hand you a moment your effort can't fix.

And when your worth is built on effort, that moment will break you.

In those moments—when your strength fails, when your solutions don't work, when your titles and trophies can't help you—ego has to either bow or bury you.

And here's a truth most won't say out loud:

Success without peace is torment.

Peace doesn't come from prominence. It comes from alignment.

So here's the real question:

Are you more focused on looking impressive than being effective?

When ego drives the narrative, we chase image over impact. We prioritize appearance over authenticity. We isolate ourselves from connection and rob ourselves of growth.

If you truly want to break free from this belief, it starts with humility.

Humility that repairs relationships.
Humility that admits when you're wrong.
Humility that says, "I don't know, but I'm willing to learn."
Humility that doesn't need the spotlight to feel seen.

This work is not easy. Choosing to deflate the ego may require you to feel the sting of exposure. It may require you to let go of the persona you've spent years crafting. But that exposure? It's not punishment. It's the doorway to peace.

Your real confidence will never be found in how high you've climbed, but in how deep you're willing to go within.

Because when you choose to be rather than just appear, you discover a version of yourself that no longer needs validation to move forward.

Simple Practice:

Ask one trusted person this question: "What's one blind spot you see in me that could limit my impact?" Write down their answer. Instead of defending yourself, sit with it. Pray through it. Let it refine you.

Remember:

Being impressive doesn't always mean you're effective.
But being effective? That's what makes you unforgettable.

CONCLUSION: TAKING BACK YOUR WEAPON

As we come to the conclusion of this chapter, I want to bring us back to something I said at the start: your inadequacy might not be proof of your deficiency. It might actually be a clue to your strength.

A few weeks ago, I was watching the movie Battleship—a film based loosely on the classic board game. There's a scene where Navy ships are at war with an alien force that makes an uninvited entrance to Earth. (Side note: if aliens really do exist, I am not ready to put on my Independence Day gear and go to war. I'd probably try to talk them into going back home. And that likely wouldn't go very well.)

Anyway, in this scene, the Navy launches a missile that doesn't just hit the enemy ship's hull—it hits the weapon system. I sat there thinking: What a brilliant place to aim. Not the bow. Not the control room. The weapon.

Because when you hit the weapon, you take away the power to strike.

And in that moment, it hit me.

What if we're in a war we can't fully see?

A war not over territory or titles, but over our significance. A war being waged against your purpose. A war where the enemy doesn't aim for your heart, your head, or your hustle—but for your weapon.

What if every time you feel inadequate, insecure, or unworthy, it's not a sign of your weakness, but evidence that your strength is being targeted? Because if you never activate your weapon, you never walk in your impact.

Let me go even deeper.

What if inadequacy is the strategy of the adversary to cause you to question the very thing that makes you powerful?

This isn't just a physical battle. It's spiritual. It's psychological. It's internal. The enemy's mission is to attack what you were created to wield—your uniqueness, your gift, your voice, your power.

If the attack can cause you to see your strength as a liability, you'll never use it. And if you never use it, you never win.

So maybe that thing you've been doubting—that you've been questioning, shrinking, criticizing, hiding—is actually the place of your greatest weaponry.

What if your greatest impact is on the other side of the very thing you've labeled "not enough"?

Let me say it plainly:

Inadequacy is a deceptive plot against your true identity.

Today, you don't just break free from limiting beliefs—you take back your weapon.

And when you do, you don't just change your life.

You change everything your life touches.

PART TWO

BREAK YOUR PATTERNS

CHAPTER FIVE

WHEN NORMAL ISN'T HEALTHY

A S   I   B E G I N this chapter, I can't help but think about my journey to this point and the different phases of life I've walked through—phases that, in hindsight, were first evolutionary and now revolutionary. I didn't just move from one physical location to another; I moved from one realization to the next about my gifts, talents, purpose, calling, and specific contribution to impacting this world.

When I look back over my life, certain moments stand out as monumental in how they radically shifted my belief system, and as my beliefs changed, my behaviors eventually followed. I talk a lot about transformation, but if I had to encapsulate it in a single thought, it would be this:

Transformation is a profound shift in our beliefs that create ripple effects in our behaviors and outcomes.

In order to change our behavior in ways that truly impact our results, the work has to start at the belief level.

There is one specific moment in my life that became a catalyst for one of the biggest shifts I've experienced. I was sitting one morning in deep introspection, thinking about areas in my life, my performance, and my value that I could improve. In that quiet space, an overwhelming thought rose up and turned into a deep, unsettling question:

Could my own acceptance be the barrier to my elevation?

I wrestled with that revelation, because I felt like I was standing at the edge of a truth that was fighting to break free inside me. That first question opened the door to an even greater one—a question that changed my outlook on life, shifted me at the belief level, and radically altered my behaviors and outcomes.

Here's the question, and I want you to lean in with me:

What am I embracing in my life as normal that is conflicting my desires or my desired state?

I believe that if you ask this question with the right heart, the right posture, and a real desire to unravel and be transparent, it can change everything for you.

I want to spend some time unpacking this. I don't just believe in this question intellectually; I believe in it experientially. In my own life, it has been a catalyst for transformation.

Let's start with the first part: What am I embracing in my life as normal…

If you have a notepad near you, write the question down and underline that phrase: embracing in my life as normal. Because so much of what we accept or reject in our lives is directly connected to what we embrace as normal.

Our norms set the tone.

Many times, it's not simply that things are happening to us because of random circumstance. Often, what keeps happening is connected to what we continually choose to accept. And we're not just accepting it—we're embracing it as our norm.

This concept of embracing norms, and how that sets the tone for what we are willing to accept or reject, is foundational to a deeper level of awareness. There are specific things in our lives that we normalize that directly conflict with our true desires or desired state.

One of the things we have far more power over than we like to admit is this: we have power over what we choose to embrace as normal. Your norms can feel right to you and still not be good for you.

Let's go deeper.

A person who views poverty as their norm—who embraces poverty as normal—can never become wealthy. Not because they can't, but because they won't. If your norm is living in a dysfunctional state, you will always sabotage your peace. If your norm is "I always have a problem to solve," you may find yourself searching for, or even unconsciously creating, problems just to solve them and feel a sense of purpose.

It breaks my heart to say this, but it's a reality: if it is your norm to live in an abusive relationship, you will justify the behaviors of the other person. You will wrap their fists, their words, their insults in a gift box and call it love.

Here is what I want you to understand as the foundation of this chapter:

- Whatever you choose to normalize, you will rationalize.
- Whatever you rationalize, you will eventually actualize.

I am passionate about this question and this concept because they opened my eyes to realize I wasn't getting out of life what I was simply asking for; I was getting out of life what I was willing to accept.

So before we go any deeper, let me ask you again:

What are you embracing in your life as normal that is conflicting your desires or your desired state?

What habits, behaviors, or responses are you continuously justifying as "your personality," "just the way you're wired," or "just who you are"—when, in reality, they are inaccurate labels causing you to reject what you truly want and accept what is creating a barrier to your desires?

When I hear people say, "I'm in my own way," this is what I picture. To me, it's about the norms we built during a season of survival that have now become enemies to our thriving.

I believe your life is meant to be lived, not just survived. I reject the idea that survival is the goal. I want you to thrive.

Here's an important shift: *thriving is not the evolution of surviving; it is the enemy of surviving.* Moving from surviving to thriving is not about polishing your survival state. It's about confronting and countering it with beliefs and behaviors radically different from those produced in survival.

The challenge with survival mode is that we usually invoke it as a temporary strategy to get through a difficult time or season. The danger is that, unknowingly, we end up becoming the season instead of allowing the season to shape who we are becoming. There is a distinct difference.

So as you lean into this chapter, consider the possibility that what is blocking your fulfillment is not your circumstance but your stance. Not just what you're facing, but how you're standing in it. It may be your willingness to embrace something as normal that is actually conflicting your desires or desired state.

So much of what we embrace as normal is not only connected to a *survival state*; it is also connected to a *value state*. Often, the deeper issue is not simply what others think of you, but what you believe about yourself.

When you struggle to embrace your intrinsic value—when you find it hard to believe you have essence and qualities that matter, that your life is significant, that you were created for purpose and on purpose—you will normalize things that are beneath you. Even if the circumstances surrounding your birth weren't intentional, a lack of intentionality can still produce significance. Don't let that slip past you.

You are reading this in this moment because something in you is stirring. A quiet inner voice is whispering that there is more for you—more fulfillment, more joy, more impact, more peace, more love. Maybe you haven't yet discovered what that "more" looks like. Maybe you're achieving externally but lacking internal fulfillment. Whatever the specifics, there is more.

The breakthrough you're looking for might be found in identifying the norms you are embracing—norms that feel normal to you but are not actually good for you.

One story that still fascinates me illustrates this perfectly. You may have heard it before, but lean in; I want to revisit it through this lens.

A man was once walking past an elephant camp. What he saw stopped him in his tracks. These massive elephants were tied to small stakes with thin chains. One end of the chain was tied to the stake; the other was around the elephant's leg. These enormous animals, capable of uprooting trees, were standing still, being held by something that seemed laughably weak compared to their strength.

The man knew that if the elephants truly wanted to, they could yank their legs and pull the stakes right out of the ground. Yet they didn't. They stayed there as if they were bound by an unbreakable force.

Curious, he asked the trainer, "How in the world are these huge elephants being held by such small stakes and chains?"

The trainer explained that when the elephants were babies, they were tied to those same stakes with those same chains. As young calves, they tried to pull away. They tugged and strained, but they were not yet strong enough to break free. Eventually, they stopped trying. They formed the belief that the stake and chain were stronger than they were.

So they grew up into fullsized elephants with a baby elephant belief. Even now, with the strength to break free at any moment, they stay stuck—mentally tied to an old story.

That story fascinates me, because I see so much of our lives in it. Like those elephants, many of us are still being held by something that might have been accurate in a past season—or might never have been accurate at all—but is now keeping us from freedom in the present. We have the courage, strength, and power to pull away, but we remain tied to old beliefs, past mistakes, careless words spoken over us, and failures we've already outgrown.

The deeper tragedy is that we have normalized this stuck state. We've worn it so long that we believe the freedom we desire isn't even possible for us.

So let me ask you:

Have you normalized being burned out all the time?
Have you normalized lack?
Have you normalized isolation?
Have you normalized anger?
Have you normalized heartbreak?
Have you normalized stress?
Have you normalized anxiety?

Have you embraced any state that is now conflicting your desires or desired state and blocking you from embracing new norms that would move you into a new life? If so, why?

Over the past few years, through coaching sessions, mentoring, and countless conversations, I've realized something: although I am called to help people, there is one type of person I cannot help.

You can never help a person who is infatuated with a story that suits their dysfunction.

A person with a victim mindset will never experience a sustained victory. You cannot help someone who is in love with hurting themselves. Choosing not to be better is an intentional choice to be bitter.

You cannot help a person who keeps accepting norms that don't serve them and rejecting new norms that could save them. Because here's the most important thing to understand about the why: they will always sabotage what they don't believe they deserve.

This is why trying to shift unhealthy norms in isolation rarely works—because the same mindset that built the story will keep defending it unless something or someone interrupts it.

Take a moment and sit with this.

How do you ensure that you don't become this person? And if you recognize yourself in these words, how do you begin to shift?

That story that suits your dysfunction—that narrative that tells you why it's okay to stay where you are—is often the clearest expression of unhealthy norms.

Here's the challenge: most of the time, it is incredibly difficult, maybe even impossible, to see these things clearly on your own.

I believe in the power of solitude—intentional time away to think, reflect, and reset with the purpose of returning with greater clarity and fire. Solitude is necessary. But isolation is dangerous.

Solitude and isolation can look the same on the outside—both involve being alone. But their purposes are completely different.

- Solitude is about disconnecting so you can reconnect—to God, to yourself, to your vision.
- Isolation is about disconnecting to validate inadequacy, insufficiency, and pain.

Isolation can be a breeding ground for depression. It cuts us off from relational intimacy with people who can help disrupt patterns we cannot see on our own.

At some point, breakthrough stops being a solo sport.

One of my biggest fears might sound simple, even funny, but it's real: giving an entire speech in front of a huge audience, delivering with passion, and then walking off stage only to discover a piece of kale stuck in my teeth. Or having a great conversation and needing someone to gesture that there's something on my face.

It's not just about appearance; it's what it represents to me. It means there was something obvious that I couldn't see about myself. And I needed someone close enough, and caring enough, to point it out.

That's how our lives work. There are things you simply cannot see without a mirror. It takes someone in proximity, who cares about you for you—not just for what you do—to help you see what you can't. Your own lens has been normalized to your current patterns, so you see life as it has been, not as it could be.

This is why relationships matter so much. The right relationships are not just companions; they are catalysts. They challenge us to become better versions of ourselves and to live lives of fulfillment.

Often, it takes intervention to disrupt unhealthy norms—either through relational interference (a friend, mentor, or coach who loves you enough to tell you the truth) or through adversity itself. We'll talk more about adversity later in this book, but know this: adversity grabs your attention. It forces you to analyze your life, your choices, your reactions, your responses, and invites you to extract the opportunities hidden inside it—to change, evolve, grow, improve, and become.

This chapter is a wakeup call disguised as a question. As we wrap up this first part of the journey, let me ask you one more time:

What are you embracing in your life as normal that is conflicting your desires or your desired state?

This is not an easy question. It demands introspection, authenticity, transparency, vulnerability, and courage. Because the answer you discover may require you to make disruptive changes—changes that alter relationships, routines, or environments. But the disruption is worth it.

There is no substitute for the journey to fulfillment. Fulfillment is that alignment, that peace, that sense of progress and poise—the deep knowing that you are being authentic to who you were created to be and that you are fulfilling your assignment in a way that cannot be diminished.

This revelation has not only changed what I am willing to accept; it has also been the catalyst for setting boundaries in my life—relationally, with my time, with my focus—so I can move toward the pinnacle of my purpose.

For me personally, one of the norms I had embraced was solving problems for everybody. I became the person who was always accessible whenever someone had an issue. Eventually, I even found myself looking for problems to solve, just to feel a sense of purpose. There was a season where my phone was never on silent, my calendar was never really mine, and my peace was always on backorder. I would leave conversations feeling emptied out while the people I helped walked away feeling lighter. On the outside it looked noble. On the inside it was slowly costing me my energy, my creativity, and my ability to hear myself think.

Fulfilling these unhealthy norms can give you temporary satisfaction, but ultimately they feel like sabotage, because once the temporary satisfaction leaves, you are drained, depleted, angry, or bitter. Those emotions are indicators that you are normalizing something that is costing you your most authentic essence.

When normal isn't healthy, nothing produced from that state can be consistently purposeful or positive.

A bad seed cannot produce good fruit.
A shaky foundation cannot produce a strong structure.
Unhealthy norms cannot produce a healthy life.

This is a question you may need to revisit at different points in your journey. I encourage you to do so, because you are worth the constant refinement—not to achieve perfection, but to experience peace.

And understand this: it is not just the question you ask that matters, but the authenticity of the answer you give. That authenticity creates the awareness transformation requires.

What if, for a moment, you took off the cape, put down the perceptions, and released the need to be impressive? What if you laid aside the titles and sat with just you in deep solitude, with an open heart, and finally asked yourself the question:

What am I accepting as normal that was never in the original design for my life?

If you really posture yourself with a hungry mind and a humble heart, the answers will start to show up. They won't always arrive all at once, but they will come as continuous revelation—things that were once okay to you now intruded by a new hesitation that makes you ask, "Why am I accepting this?"

And if your mind can conceive this and your heart will believe it, then your hands can begin to create the change you truly desire.

As we get ready for the next phase of your journey, know this: I'm proud of you. I'm walking with you. And I am excited for the continuous revelations ahead as you go deeper than motivation.

CHAPTER SIX

BECOMING IS THE WORK

"Everything that is alive may have life, but not
everything that has life is actually living."

IN EARLIER CHAPTERS, we named this as the tension
between existing and truly living. Now I want to show you how exposure
and a transformed mindset became my way out of that survival state.
The paradox between merely having life and truly living is so subtle
that many never recognize the difference. They move through their
days unaware—functioning on autopilot, existing but not thriving.
They get up, go to work, take care of responsibilities, and go to bed, yet
something in them knows they were made for more than this routine.

I have witnessed this firsthand—people from all walks of life who
have unknowingly subscribed to survival mode, forfeiting their right
to fully experience the richness of their existence.

Some reach this state as a byproduct of trauma—a lifealtering
event that shook them to their core, leaving them committed only to
selfpreservation. They prioritize protection over progression, shutting
themselves off from anything that could expose them to further pain.

Growth demands discomfort, and for them, the risk feels far too great, too reminiscent of past wounds. What saddens me most is that for many, their dreams die at the same moment their trauma occurs. Not a physical death, but the death of their faith, their excitement, their childlike wonder. They become spectators in their own lives, absent from the reality that they still possess the power to shape their destiny.

Others enter this state through repeated failure—pouring themselves into a business, a career move, or a bold decision, only to experience disappointment over and over again. These people still have a fight in them, but they've lost the fire. And fight without fire can make you appear impressive, but it will never make you effective. Fight without fire makes you go through the motions but doesn't bring the emotion. Fight without fire lets you settle for good but never reach for great.

And then there are those who never truly live because they have simply never been exposed to more. Exposure is the essence of possibility. It is difficult to crave what you have never seen. It is difficult to chase what you don't even know exists. This is why I believe so many people remain stuck—not because they lack talent, intelligence, or ability, but because they lack the exposure that could awaken their vision.

I know this because I could have easily been one of them.

Back home in Antigua and Barbuda, many of us shared a similar upbringing, yet ended up with vastly different realities as adults. The difference? Exposure. My parents—whether they realized it or not—exposed me to a world beyond the walls of our island. Every year, they sacrificed to take us on family vacations, flying us from the Caribbean to places like London, New York City, Georgia, and South America. Those trips weren't just vacations; they were vision trips. They expanded my understanding of what was possible. They changed my palette for life.

When a person is hit with exposure, it does something profound. Exposure creates possibility. Possibility ignites potential. Ignited potential creates a push. And that push leads to purpose. I returned home from those trips with a different perspective. It wasn't that I no longer appreciated where I came from—I did. But I had seen more, and I knew there was more. That exposure was the foundation that led me to seek education beyond my island, to connect with diverse perspectives, and ultimately, to build a life and career that stretched beyond my original environment.

So I ask you: Are you truly living, or are you just existing?

Are you moving through life with intention, or are you allowing circumstances to dictate your path? Do you have a fire and a focus for something greater, or are you merely accepting life as it is? Are you standing in front of a blank canvas, actively designing the life you want for yourself, your family, and your legacy?

I believe our greatest gift as humans is our ability to create. We were designed by a Creator with creative power inside of us. Life was never meant to be endured—it was meant to be designed, built, and fully embraced. Yet, whether by trauma, failure, or lack of exposure, many of us have unknowingly surrendered that power.

But I will tell you this: your power cannot be taken—it can only be given away.

Too many of us give our power away to adversity, to fear, to the stories we tell ourselves about why we can't or shouldn't move forward. We unconsciously create excuses that validate our need to stay comfortable. We rationalize why we are stuck instead of doing the hard work to break free.

Yet, within every person—within you—there is an unshakable power waiting to be activated. A power that is both innate (the ability to make choices and create change) and divine (the spiritual wisdom and discernment to navigate life's complexities).

If you can shift your mindset, you can shift your reality.

WHAT MINDSET REALLY IS

I have heard countless people talk about the concept of mindset. But my mind always asks a deeper question: What is mindset, really? Is it just a set of affirmations? A series of positive thoughts? A decision to stop thinking negatively? Or is it something far greater?

Carol Dweck's research on fixed vs. growth mindsets provides a strong foundation, but I simplify mindset even further:

Mindset is your mind being set on something. It is commitment—what your mind is committed to, focused on, locked into.

Some people's minds are set on growth, resilience, and success. Others' minds are set on doubt, fear, and lack. But here's what I know for sure: you don't really know where your mindset is until it's tested.

Anyone can have a strong mindset when things are going well. But adversity is the ultimate litmus test. It reveals whether your commitment is real or conditional. And I learned this the hard way.

When I lost my father to cancer, my world was shaken. I was searching for hope but couldn't find it in books, in friendships, in relationships. The only thing that anchored me was my faith, and from that faith, something powerful emerged—a voice. I started speaking words that were stronger than my circumstances. I spoke about hope, impact, and transformation—not because I had fully grasped them yet, but because I needed them.

At first, I thought I was inspiring others. But the truth is, I was talking to myself while the world listened. Every word I spoke had to come through me, which meant it had to impact me first. That's when I learned the true power of mindset—not just as a concept, but as a force that could literally shift my reality.

Mindset is not revealed in comfort; it is revealed in struggle. I believed I had a strong mindset—until I found myself struggling financially while trying to build a speaking career. I was inspiring others but silently negotiating with my phone company not to cut off my service. I was delivering powerful keynotes while privately battling discouragement, asking myself: How can I teach others to thrive when I feel like I'm barely surviving?

That season exposed something deep: my confidence was tied to my financial security, not my purpose. When things were good, I felt unstoppable. But when adversity hit, I shrank back. And that is when I realized the truth—commitment that is never tested cannot be trusted.

Your mindset is not proven in easy moments. It is proven when life challenges everything you thought you knew. But the beauty of adversity is this: it is the greatest teacher of who you really are.

So, what is your mind set on?

This is where we begin the journey of going Deeper Than Motivation—because motivation is fleeting, but a transformed mindset lasts forever.

THE 7 PRINCIPLES OF AN UNSHAKABLE MINDSET

(and the 7 Phases of My Journey)

As I advanced in my life and career, I realized something critical: the gap between theory and practice is where most people get stuck.

Profundity is essential, but practicality is paramount. It's not enough to know something—you must be able to apply it in real time, in the real world, in real circumstances.

That's why I'm not just giving you concepts. I'm giving you principles. Seven of them.

These seven mindset principles are not just ideas; they are a pathway—one that leads you from uncertainty to being unstoppable. Each principle builds upon the last, creating a momentum that takes you from clarity to confidence to influence, and ultimately, to impact.

I don't believe in a onesizefitsall approach. Because the truth is, there is no such thing.

We all come from different backgrounds, different circumstances, different resources, different struggles. No singular solution can apply to everyone. That's why I teach in frameworks.

A framework is not a rigid rulebook. It's a set of guiding principles—principles rooted in experience, psychology, and philosophy, backed by years of study, personal discovery, and realworld application. This framework will not give you a stepbystep checklist for life, but what it will do is equip you with the tools to navigate life powerfully, no matter where you are, what you have, or what you are facing.

These seven principles will change the way you think, the way you operate, and ultimately, the way you show up in the world.

They will first help you gain unshakable clarity—because without clarity, you cannot move forward with power.

That clarity will then produce a deep confidence—a confidence that is not circumstantial, but rooted in truth.

And confidence is the secret ingredient to maximizing influence—because you cannot lead, inspire, or impact at the highest level without first believing in yourself.

And finally, influence is proportionate to impact.

When you master your mindset, you master your ability to lead, to create, and to transform the world around you. So here we go!

PRINCIPLE 1:
AWARENESS: YOU CANNOT HEAL WHAT YOU HIDE.

The first step to transformation is awareness. You cannot change what you refuse to confront. Earlier in this book, we talked about the power of reflection and the danger of shame; this principle is where that reflection becomes intentional, honest illumination.

Too often, we suppress the very things that are holding us back. We ignore our insecurities, dismiss our fears, and sidestep the hard conversations that could lead to our breakthrough. But whatever you bury alive will always resurrect itself in your life.

Limiting beliefs thrive in the shadows. They show up when you're about to take a risk, whispering, Who do you think you are? They creep in when you're on the verge of greatness, reminding you of every failure, every setback, every mistake.

To eliminate these limitations, you must first bring them into the light. Identify them. Name them. Call them out. If you struggle with believing in your own value, ask yourself: Where did this belief come from? Who told me I wasn't enough? Often, the limitations we carry are just repetitions of someone else's broken perspective—a perspective we have unknowingly accepted as truth.

But here's the good news: if a belief can be learned, it can be unlearned. And if it can be unlearned, it can be replaced with something greater.

Many of us struggle with selftransparency. We live in a world where we constantly wear masks to be understood, accepted, or embraced by others. I call this mask our representative—the version of ourselves that we hire to show the world. The version we believe others will approve of.

Some of us have a representative at work. A different one in our friendships. Another in our relationships. We show up as who we think we should be, not who we truly are.

But the danger of always performing is that eventually, you forget which version of you is real. When you're alone, do you know who's speaking—the authentic you, or the one who's still stuck in "acting mode"?

Selftransparency is the key to getting to the root of what's actually happening in your life.

Because in every challenge, we are dealing with one of two things:

1. The fruit of the problem (the symptoms—what we see on the surface).
2. The root of the problem (the real issue hiding beneath the surface).

Most people focus on fruit problems—getting angry at their kids, blowing up in traffic, selfsabotaging opportunities. But those are just reactions. The real work is root work.

- The fruit: You snap at your kids or your team.
- The root: You're overworked, undervalued, and resentful that you have no space for yourself.
- The fruit: You curse out the driver who cuts you off.
- The root: You suppress your emotions so much in life that road rage becomes your only outlet.
- The fruit: You procrastinate on launching your business.
- The root: You fear failure because you don't feel "enough."

Real transformation begins when we stop managing fruit problems and start digging into root problems.

THE DOCTOR'S OFFICE ANALOGY: HOW WE GET TO THE ROOT

Think about what happens when you visit the doctor. Before the doctor even sees you, a nurse asks you a series of general questions.

- What's going on today?
- Where are you feeling discomfort?
- How long have you been experiencing this?

The questions start broad, then become more specific as they narrow in on the real issue. But the doctor's ability to diagnose isn't just based on their expertise—it's based on your honesty. If you lie about your symptoms, the diagnosis will be inaccurate. If you downplay the pain, they won't see the urgency.

Most of us don't get the answers we need in life because we're not asking the right questions and we're not answering honestly.

- We tell people we're "fine" when we're drowning.
- We say "it's okay" when it's not.
- We say "I'm handling it" when we're barely holding on.

This is where our representative shows up again—the one who convinces us to suppress, deny, and avoid. But avoidance is a false protector. It doesn't remove the problem—it just delays the consequences.

WHY WE FEAR ILLUMINATION

Sometimes, the thing that will free you is also the thing that terrifies you.

When we illuminate something, we can no longer ignore it. And that means we have to deal with it. That's why some people choose to stay blind.

But staying blind doesn't make the danger disappear.

- Some people get burned by the stove once—and never go back in the kitchen.
- Some people experience failure—and never take another risk.
- Some people experience heartbreak—and shut themselves off from love.

We avoid what hurt us in the past because we think distance equals safety. But true freedom isn't about avoidance—it's about confrontation.

You cannot heal what you refuse to reveal.

And the reality is, your breakthrough might look like the thing that once broke you.

- If money once crushed you, your breakthrough might be in building wealth.
- If failure once paralyzed you, your breakthrough might be in taking bold risks.
- If love once hurt you, your breakthrough might be in learning to love again.

Your next level will always require you to face what you fear, not flee from it.

THE PATH TO ILLUMINATION AND ELIMINATION

So how do we illuminate the things that have been limiting us?

Step 1: Get into Solitude.

Real selftransparency requires intentional disconnection from distractions. This could be a few hours, a few days, or even a few weeks—but it must be a dedicated space for honest reflection.

Step 2: Ask Hard Questions.

Use introspective questions to bring hidden thoughts into the light:

- Where am I in life right now?
- How did I get here?
- What patterns keep repeating in my life?
- What beliefs do I hold that might be limiting me?
- What fears am I refusing to confront?

Step 3: Identify the Root, Not Just the Fruit.

Every struggle has a root cause. Instead of asking, "Why do I keep failing?", ask, "What belief, habit, or fear is keeping me in this cycle?"

Step 4: Own the Truth Without Shame.

Illumination isn't about selfcondemnation—it's about selfawareness. It's not about saying, "I'm broken," but rather, "I see where I need to heal."

Step 5: Take the First Step.

Awareness without action is useless. Once you illuminate an issue, commit to one action that moves you toward eliminating it.

Illumination is not easy. It requires courage. It requires honesty. But what you refuse to face today will control you tomorrow.

I stand as living proof that you can eliminate what has been limiting you—but only when you first bring it into the light.

If you want to transform your life, you must make one bold decision:

Stop running. Turn on the light. Face the truth.

Because what you illuminate, you can eliminate or let me say it a different way - you cannot heal what you hide.

PRINCIPLE 2:
OWNERSHIP: YOUR LIFE IS YOUR RESPONSIBILITY.

At some point, you must realize that your life is your responsibility. Your success is on you. Your growth is on you. Your healing is on you. In Chapter One, when I shared about speaking hope with a negative bank account, that tension pushed me into this phase of taking extreme ownership.

The moment you stop blaming external factors for your internal stagnation is the moment you step into true power.

This is not about ignoring challenges or pretending circumstances don't exist. It is about refusing to let them control you. There will always be reasons why you could stay where you are. But there will always be greater reasons why you must move forward.

You are not a product of your environment; you are a product of your decisions. I've heard this powerful African proverb that says you may have been born looking like your daddy, but you'll die looking like your decisions. The most powerful decision you can make today is to take full ownership of your future.

OWNERSHIP: THE BRIDGE BETWEEN WHAT IS AND WHAT COULD BE

Building on Principle 1—that in order to eliminate it, you must illuminate it—this principle is the natural next step.

Awareness without ownership cannot produce progress.

Ownership is the bridge between where you are and where you could be. Without ownership, we would not know the greats of our time. Because the truth is, most people who have achieved greatness did not look like where they came from.

Let's take basketball as an example. Now, some of you may put this book down after reading this, but LeBron James is the greatest basketball player of all time. Walk with me on this. His accomplishments on the court are undeniable, but what fascinates me more is his life off the court.

I haven't met LeBron yet (yet—because maybe he'll read this book one day), but as a man and father, I'm deeply inspired by what he has built. His upbringing didn't define his outcome—his ownership did. His lack created a desire, and that desire became the foundation for a life radically different from his childhood experiences.

And this is what we see in so many of the greats: they took ownership of their reality and made a decision to shift their lives—despite their circumstances.

THE DEFINITION OF OWNERSHIP

Ownership, at its core, is the moment when you embrace this absolute truth:

"It is nobody else's fault. And it is nobody else's responsibility. If it is to be, it is up to me."

This is easier said than done. Because taking ownership means letting go of the stories we have told ourselves about why we can't move forward.

And here's the truth: we love our stories. We become so committed to them that we fail to see that our story is the very thing keeping us stuck.

Some people have built their entire identity around:

- Being a single parent.
- Growing up in poverty.
- Not having a formal education.
- Coming from a broken home.

The facts may be real—but they do not have to be your truth.

Yes, your story impacted you, but it does not have to define you.

And here is the greatest challenge with ownership: once you take full responsibility, you can no longer use your story as an excuse.

EXCUSES ARE COMFORT, BUT COMFORT IS A CRUTCH

The opposite of ownership is excuses.

Excuses allow us to blame people, circumstances, and external forces for why we are not where we want to be. And while they may feel justified, they ultimately act as a crutch that prevents us from stepping into transformation.

Most of the world's problems aren't actually the problems—they are a lackofownership problem.

Think about it:

- What would happen if two people in conflict took full ownership of their actions?

- What would change if corporations took ownership over how they prioritize profit over people?
- How different would our world be if leadership, government, and organizations operated from ownership instead of excuses?

Lack of ownership today becomes a curse for the next generation.

The best relationships, businesses, and personal transformations happen when people take full ownership—not just for their results, but for their reactions, their patterns, and their future.

THE SHIFT FROM "I SHOULD" TO "I WILL"

When we live without ownership, we live in the land of "I should."

- I should start that business.
- I should change my habits.
- I should forgive.
- I should improve my mindset.

"I should" keeps you in limbo. It is a delayed decision that creates space for doubt, fear, and stagnation.

But ownership shifts us from "I should" to "I will."

- I will take action.
- I will make the change.
- I will take full responsibility for my next step.

And "I will" is where power lives.

ACTION STEP: TAKE OWNERSHIP TODAY

Let's apply this principle right now.

1. Identify one area of your life that needs improvement.

2. What steps need to be taken to improve it?

3. What can you control and execute relentlessly?

These questions are the beginning of a cadence of ownership.

But let me give you a deeper truth: most people only take ownership reactively. Meaning, they only take responsibility when life forces them into a corner. When an opportunity appears or pain demands change.

Real power is in proactive ownership.

THE INTERSECTION OF PREPARATION AND OPPORTUNITY

There are two forces that shape destiny: Preparation and Opportunity.

- Preparation is what you control.
- Opportunity is what you don't.

Opportunity is never guaranteed, but preparation is always in your hands.

Growing up, my father was a huge fan of motivational speakers. He listened to Dr. Myles Munroe, Zig Ziglar, T.D. Jakes, and Les Brown. And there's one thing Les Brown said that my father repeated to me daily:

"It's better to be prepared for an opportunity that never comes than to have an opportunity come and not be prepared."

That truth has stuck with me for life.

If you are not taking ownership, you are not preparing. And if you are not preparing, you will miss the opportunity when it comes.

The moment you eliminate excuses and take extreme ownership over your mindset, your habits, and your future—you shift the trajectory of your life.

FINAL THOUGHT: IF IT'S TO BE, IT'S UP TO ME

A life without ownership is a life of cycles. A life where we keep blaming, waiting, and wishing instead of changing, deciding, and executing.

If it is to be, it is up to you.

Say it. Write it down. Let it sink in.

Ownership is the key to transformation.

PRINCIPLE 3:
IDENTITY: YOUR NORMS BECOME YOUR NARRATIVE.

I actually believe the genesis of my transformation began with a single question—one that I now challenge my coaches, mentees, and audience members to consider deeply. It may seem simple at first glance, but it carries profound significance. This question became the catalyst to my contribution, the turning point of my transformation, the launchpad to my legacy:

What have I normalized in my life that is actually conflicting with my desires—or my desired state?

Earlier, in Chapter Five, we started asking what you've been embracing as normal in your life. This principle takes that same question and applies it directly to your identity.

You see, this question may sound ordinary, but it cuts deep. It forces you to confront what you've allowed to become familiar, even if that familiarity is keeping you bound. It confronts your existing norms—the silent agreements you've made with mediocrity, dysfunction, or fear. These norms, often adopted without question, become the guardrails of what we're willing to accept or reject in our lives.

THE HIDDEN POWER OF NORMS

Some of us have normalized burnout, always being tired. Some have normalized giving the most to others and leaving the least for ourselves. Some have normalized struggling financially, never soaring. Some have normalized moving from dysfunction to dysfunction, never finding peace.

The danger? We tolerate what we normalize. And when you tolerate dysfunction long enough, it starts to feel like truth.

You don't lack the capacity to transform—you lack the willingness to challenge what you've normalized.

So let me ask you again: What have you normalized in your life that is conflicting with your desires?

THE ROOT OF OUR NORMS: THE 4 E'S

To truly unpack what you've normalized, you have to understand the 4 E's that shape your belief system:

1. Experiences
2. Exposure
3. Environment
4. Essence

These shape your core beliefs, and your core beliefs drive your perception. Your perception influences your actions. Your actions produce your results. And your results reinforce your beliefs.

Let's break them down:

1. Experiences

Your experiences shape how you perceive yourself, others, and the world. Two people can look at the same situation and see something completely different—not because of the thing itself, but because of what it reminds them of, what it echoes from their past.

Ask yourself: What experiences have shaped my perception of what's normal? And are those perceptions accurate—or just familiar?

2. Exposure

Exposure is the information you absorb—from books, videos, conversations, culture, or media. It's what you've been shown is possible.

I shared earlier how being exposed to the world outside my Caribbean island changed me. It showed me there was more—and that "more" rewired my belief system.

Imagine a highrise building in Dallas. Someone living on the 2nd floor hears street noise, sees traffic, and feels tension. Someone on the 48th floor sees the skyline, feels peace, and has a broader view.

Same building. Different floors. Different exposures. Different realities.

3. Environment

Your environment either reinforces your beliefs or challenges them. Most people gravitate toward environments that reinforce what they already believe—because it's comfortable.

I'll never forget the first time I played golf at a private course. Before that, I thought public courses were luxurious. But that experience upgraded my entire perspective. Suddenly, my palette changed.

That's what happens when your environment challenges your norm—it stretches your vision.

4. Essence

Your essence is your wiring—your unique genetic makeup, how your brain processes the world, how you show up.

Understanding your essence helps you recognize how your natural tendencies influence your norms. Some of us are wired to be highly empathetic, others more logical. Some move fast, some need silence.

When you expect others to share your norms, you create unnecessary conflict. But when you analyze your own essence, you unlock your personal formula for growth.

THE TRAP OF RATIONALIZATION

Here's where it gets even deeper: you will always rationalize what you normalize.

Why? Because your identity is tied to your norm.

- "I always struggle financially"—becomes a belief.
- "I never do well in relationships"—becomes an identity.
- "I give the most to others and never receive support"—becomes a narrative you cling to.

Rationalization is how we protect our norms—even when they're hurting us.

People will find comfort in chaos if that's what they know.

Peace may feel unsafe. Stability may feel boring. Abundance may feel fake.

This is not about shame. It's about selfawareness. And selfawareness is the doorway to freedom.

YOUR NORMS ARE NOT NEUTRAL

This principle flows directly from Principle 2 (Ownership). You cannot change your life until you first acknowledge that your norms may be the biggest thing in your way.

What if the thing you keep calling "normal" is actually the biggest threat to your purpose? What if you've built your home in dysfunction because it's all you've ever known?

Here's what I want you to do:

Your Action Framework

1. Identify the Cycles.

- What patterns keep repeating in your life?
- Are you always struggling in relationships? Always stuck financially? Always anxious?

2. Name the Beliefs.

- What do you believe about yourself, others, or the world that fuels this cycle?

3. Analyze the 4 E's.

- Experiences: What events shaped this belief?
- Exposure: What ideas, books, or people reinforced it?
- Environment: Who do you surround yourself with?
- Essence: How might your wiring influence your default response?

4. Establish New Beliefs.

- What new belief would align with your desired outcome?
- What new exposure, environment, or experience could help reinforce it?

What you call "normal" becomes your personal ceiling. But you were never meant to live under a low ceiling. You were created to rise. Transformation doesn't begin with action—it begins with belief. And you can't believe differently until you first question what you've been calling normal.

Your new life will cost you your old norms. Are you ready to let them go?

PRINCIPLE 4:
DOUBT THRIVES IN DOUBLE-MINDEDNESS

The number one killer of destiny is distraction—the kind that pulls you in multiple directions and keeps you from standing in the definitive clarity required to walk into your calling. That kind of distraction causes destruction. And destruction begins with something far more subtle: doubt.

I remember my first year of entrepreneurship. I had just launched my consulting business, helping organizations achieve transformative excellence through culture, collaboration, and contribution. On paper, that first year was successful—I earned just under $100,000. But despite the external results, I knew deep down that I had not given it my all.

Not because I didn't care. Not because I lacked passion. Not because I wasn't grateful.

But because hidden inside my drive was a tumor called doubt.

I call it a tumor because that's how dangerous it is. It starts small, subtle—uncertainty here, hesitation there. But it grows. It spreads. And if left unchecked, it will destroy the very thing it was placed inside of.

THE SUBTLE POWER OF DOUBT

Here's the truth: doubt is human. It's the natural byproduct of facing the unknown. But doubt becomes toxic when it evolves from a moment of hesitation to a mindset of hesitation—when it doesn't just visit us but takes residence inside us.

Doubt is what turns capable people into hesitant people. Doubt is what takes dreams and shelves them. Doubt is what creates paralysis in people with powerful potential.

The most dangerous kind of doubt is the kind that leads to double-mindedness.

If I could give one piece of advice to my younger self, it would be simple, and it's taken from what I believe is the greatest book ever written—the Bible:

"Let your yes be yes, and your no be no."

Double-mindedness is when you straddle the line. When your yes isn't fully yes. When your no isn't fully no. When you say you're committed but operate like you're just curious.

Doubt is the breeding ground for fear. Doubt is the fuel source for insecurity. Doubt is the catalyst for paralysis.

And nothing of significance is ever built in a mind divided.

I've always said it's better to be loud, strong, and dead wrong than quiet, hesitant, and never begin. That's because doubt disrupts momentum. And when you live in a constant internal negotiation, nothing moves.

FAITH VS. DOUBT

Everything great requires faith.

Faith is the internal fire for something you haven't seen yet. Doubt is the fire extinguisher for that flame.

Now don't confuse healthy doubt—which leads to learning and growth—with the kind of doubt that leads to double-mindedness.

Double-mindedness is when you do while doubting. It's when you speak while second-guessing.

It's when you show up physically but are checked out mentally.

In my speaker training program Speak with Conviction, I teach a core principle: "In your head, you're dead." Because the moment you start analyzing your worth while trying to express it, you've already muted your own impact.

THE DANGER OF GRAY

You're either in or you're out. You're either going forward or standing still. Gray—the middle ground—is the most dangerous place to live. It's not a yes. It's not a no. It's a delay disguised as safety.

Most of what you're praying for, hoping for, and working toward... won't show up until you

show up.

Because waiting for certainty before committing isn't faith. It's fear dressed as caution.

4 LEVELS OF COMMITMENT

If you want to break free from double-mindedness, you must make an unshakable commitment to four areas:

1. Commitment to the Promise

- Are you fully committed to the outcome you desire?
- Or are you just curious until it gets hard?

2. Commitment to the Process

- Are you willing to grow, fail, learn, stretch, and evolve?
- Will you sacrifice comfort for progress?

3. Commitment to the Path

- Are you willing to walk your unique journey—not someone else's version of success?
- Can you own your pace, your process, and your rhythm?

4. Commitment to the Pruning

- Can you embrace the refining?
- Can you allow failure to shape you and maturity to develop you?

You see, most people want the promise, but not the process. Some embrace the process, but not their unique path. Many walk the path, but resist the pruning.

And if you're double-minded about any of these, you will delay the very thing you're destined to do.

If you're struggling with doubt, ask yourself:

- Am I really committed—or just curious?
- Am I all in—or waiting to see how it goes?
- Am I saying yes with my mouth—but living no with my actions?

If you want to ignite your purpose, you must make a definitive decision to show up.

Say yes. Loudly. Say no. Boldly.

Because doubt thrives in the in-between. And a double-minded person will always be unstable in all their ways. Let your yes be YES. Let your no be NO. And watch how clarity creates momentum, and momentum transforms your life.

PRINCIPLE 5:
YOU MUST CHOOSE VISION OVER VALIDATION

There is a battle that takes place in every person's mind—a battle between vision and validation.

Vision is the dream. The purpose. The calling. Validation is the craving for external confirmation. The need for applause before action. The desire to be seen before stepping forward.

And too often, validation wins.

Too often, people abandon vision for validation. They trade what is possible for what is predictable. They settle for a life that's acceptable rather than a life that's exceptional.

Why?

Because validation is safe. It's familiar. It strokes the ego and whispers the illusion of support.

But here's what I've learned: The people assigned to validate your vision will not show up until you start walking in it. No one will believe in you at the level you desire until you believe in you—deeply, unwaveringly, and without the need for a round of applause.

If you always need a green light from someone else, you will forever live at the pace of their permission. And if you are waiting for permission to become great, you will be waiting forever.

VISION IS A PULLING FORCE

Vision is not just an idea—it's a pulling force. It drags you into your destiny, yanks you toward purpose, and draws out what's been buried deep inside you.

And vision is never passive.

A vision should include what I call the 3 C's:

1. Clarity of Vision

- You must know what you're aiming for. Not in vague terms, but with sharpness and specificity. What do you want to build? Who do you want to impact? What does "done" look like?

2. Connection to Vision

- Your vision must matter to you. It can't be just a trendy pursuit or a borrowed ambition. Connection means it's rooted in your story, your pain, your promise. For me, much of my vision is fueled by the impact my late father had on my life—and how I want to carry that same transformative power into the lives of others.

3. Conviction By Vision

- This is what comes after you start. Conviction is born through impact. It's when your story touches someone else's life and their eyes well up with gratitude. Conviction is what keeps you going when motivation wears off. It turns your vision from an idea into a responsibility.

If one of these is missing, your vision lacks weight. If two are missing, your vision is fragile.

And if all three are present, your vision becomes unshakable.

THE PARADOX OF VISION

Here's the paradox: vision always starts internally. You feel it before you see it. You sense it before it makes sense. And that can be incredibly disorienting. You see the vision. You feel its weight. You hear its call.

But no one else does.

And because you're alone in that seeing… you start searching for confirmation. You want someone else to say, "Yes, I see it too."

That's where validation creeps in.

We try to anchor what we feel internally by seeking a yes externally.

But here's the danger: validation often comes from people who cannot see the vision the way you see it. And why would they? The vision didn't come to them. It came to you.

FILTERING VISION THROUGH BROKEN LENSES

Every person sees through the lens of their experience. And when you ask someone to validate your vision, what you're really doing is handing them your glasses.

But what if their lenses are cracked? What if their prescription was never meant to match your eyesight?

When they put on your glasses—or worse, when you put on theirs—everything will look distorted. Not because it is broken, but because they're looking through a broken frame.

This is why filtering your vision through the lens of someone else's validation can shrink your dream.

Let me be clear: there's a difference between validation and consultation.

- Validation says, "You're good enough."
- Consultation says, "Here's how to sharpen your approach."

We need wise counsel, not constant affirmation. We need feedback, not approval.

THE FEAR BENEATH THE NEED

Most validation-seeking behavior is rooted in fear. Specifically, three types:

1. Fear of Illness or Death
2. Fear of Poverty or Loss
3. Fear of Criticism

It's the third one—fear of criticism—that chokes out vision the fastest. We're afraid to be seen building something that others might not understand. So we wait for a yes. For applause. For safety.

But the truth is, most people won't understand your vision until it becomes their reality.

So yes, your journey may feel lonely at times. There may be silence when you expected cheers.

But it's in those quiet moments that your conviction is forged. When no one is watching, you become who you need to be when everyone finally sees.

Vision doesn't always come with praise.

Sometimes, it comes with confusion. Sometimes, it comes with doubt. Sometimes, it comes with people saying, "You've changed."

But if you're building something bold, something real, something that transcends the moment—you must learn to be okay with the silence. With the questions. With the side-eyes.

Because you were never building it for applause. You were building it for impact.

And impact takes time.

PRACTICAL APPLICATION:
HOW TO CHOOSE VISION OVER VALIDATION

1. Clarify Before You Magnify

Write the vision. Sit with it. Map it out. Before you start announcing it to the world, make sure it's strong enough to stand. Too many people expose their vision in its infancy and let others poke holes before it even has a backbone. Don't let others knead your dough before it rises.

2. Test the Voice

Only share your vision with people who have context. People who have built something. People who understand the weight of building. Stop trying to get blueprints from people who've never built anything. They mean well—but their lack of clarity will cloud your certainty.

3. Schedule Solitude

Regularly step away from the noise. Revisit your vision in silence. Ask:

- Is this still aligned?
- Have I watered it down?
- Am I building from my heart—or from someone else's opinion?

Solitude is where realignment happens.

Think of it like a vehicle alignment. A slight drift today becomes a major detour tomorrow. Realign early. Realign often.

THE VISION CAME TO YOU FOR A REASON

You are the vessel. Your gift. Your story. Your struggle. Your strength. If it had been meant for someone else, they would've seen it.

But it came to you.

So remember this:

- The vision will come to you.
- The validation may come through others.
- But the execution can only come from you.

Be cautious of applause that's louder than your assignment. Be careful of praise that dilutes your purpose.

Choose vision. Choose clarity. Choose conviction.

And let the validation catch up when it does.

Your yes is enough.

PRINCIPLE 6:
CONNECTION: ALIGNMENT OVER ACCESS.

All through this book, we've talked about the power of environment and exposure. This principle is where that truth becomes personal, relational, and practical.

The reality is, you cannot connect deeply to what is next if you stay entangled with everything from what was. You cannot fully hold onto your future while clinging with both hands to every piece of your past. Connection always comes with a cost: something has to be released so something greater can be received.

Many of us want purposefilled relationships, lifegiving environments, and rooms that stretch us—but we don't want to disconnect from old patterns, old circles, and old versions of ourselves. We want new fruit on the same tree.

Connection demands alignment.

THE MYTH OF "I CAN STAY THE SAME AND STILL GO HIGHER"

One of the greatest lies we tell ourselves is, "I can keep all of my current habits, relationships, and rhythms—and still step fully into my next level." We don't say it out loud, but we live like it.

We try to carry everyone and everything with us into every season. We feel guilty for outgrowing conversations that used to entertain us but no longer nourish us. We apologize for needing more depth, more honesty, more accountability.

But here's the truth: you are not called to abandon people, but you are called to be a good steward of your assignment. And stewardship sometimes means redefining access.

- Some relationships are for a reason.
- Some are for a season.
- Some are for a lifetime.

Confusion comes when we try to make "reason" relationships into "lifetime" relationships simply because we're afraid of being misunderstood.

CONNECTION REQUIRES CLARITY

Connection is not just about being surrounded by people. It's about being surrounded by the right people—those who challenge you, sharpen you, and call you into who you're becoming.

Ask yourself:

- Who in my life calls out the best in me, not just the busiest in me?
- Who can tell me the truth—even when it's inconvenient—because they care more about my becoming than my comfort?
- Who do I feel smaller around, and who do I feel stretched around?

The answers to those questions reveal a lot about your current connections.

You were not designed to do life alone. We said earlier that solitude is powerful but isolation is dangerous. This is where connection becomes the antidote to isolation. The right relationships function like mirrors and catalysts: they show you what you can't see, and they push you beyond what you'd do on your own.

DISCONNECTION WITH HONOR

Disconnecting from misaligned connections is not about arrogance; it's about alignment. It's about acknowledging that every room is not your room, and every voice is not your voice.

Sometimes that looks like:

- Creating new boundaries around your time and energy.

- Choosing not to engage certain conversations that always pull you back into old mindsets.
- Allowing certain relationships to shift roles—moving from inner circle to acquaintance without bitterness.

You can honor the past while still protecting your future.

The key is this: don't demonize what you're distancing from. Bless it for what it was, learn what you needed to learn, and then step forward. When you disconnect with honor, you leave the door open for reconciliation, but you don't leave your destiny hostage to it.

ROOMS THAT MATCH YOUR NEXT

Connection is also about where you place yourself.

- Rooms of growth.
- Rooms of accountability.
- Rooms of excellence.
- Rooms where your gift isn't just tolerated, but trusted.

You can't keep hiding in rooms where you're the most comfortable and expect to expand. There must be rooms where you are not the smartest person in the room, where the standard is higher than what you're used to, where mediocrity is not an option.

When you choose connection with intention, you give your future self the gift of context. You make it harder to shrink back, because your environment keeps reminding you of who you really are.

To connect to the life you're called to, you will have to disconnect from the life that's draining you.

PRINCIPLE 7:
EXECUTION: FOCUSED ACTION CREATES TRACTION.

By the time you arrive at this principle, you've already done a lot of internal work. You've illuminated what needed to be seen. You've taken ownership. You've confronted your norms and begun to shift your identity. You've disempowered doubt. You've chosen vision over validation. You've started aligning your connections.

Now the question becomes simple and sobering:

What will you do with all of this?

At this point, the real battle is not for more information or more inspiration. The real battle is for your focus.

DISTRACTION: THE SILENT THIEF

Distraction rarely shows up waving red flags. It comes disguised as good things that are not your thing. It shows up as endless options, constant comparison, and the subtle pull to do everything except the one thing that would actually move your life forward.

You can be busy and still be offpurpose.

You can be productive and still be unfulfilled.

You can have a full calendar and an empty soul.

Focus is not about doing more. Focus is about doing what matters—on purpose, repeatedly.

Ask yourself:

- What are the few assignments in this season that God has actually placed in my hands?

- What are the distractions that consistently pull me away from those assignments?
- What stories do I tell myself to justify those distractions?

The answers to those questions will reveal whether your life is being led by intention or by interruption.

THE POWER OF FOCUSED EXECUTION

Execution is where your internal shifts become external evidence.

Execution looks like:

- Blocking time on your calendar and protecting it as fiercely as you protect other people's meetings.
- Finishing the project you started instead of chasing a new idea every time it gets hard.
- Practicing the skills connected to your calling—even on days when you don't feel inspired.
- Creating systems and rhythms that support your focus instead of constantly relying on willpower.

You don't rise to the level of your intentions; you fall to the level of your patterns. Focused execution is how you build new patterns.

SAYING NO ON PURPOSE

If focus is going to be your reality, "no" has to become a holy word in your vocabulary.

- No to assignments that dilute your impact.
- No to conversations that drain your energy.
- No to opportunities that look good but don't align with your vision.
- No to the version of you that feels safer but smaller.

Every yes is expensive. When you say yes to one thing, you are automatically saying no to something else. Focus forces you to count the cost—before your calendar counts it for you.

You are not selfish for protecting your focus. You are a steward.

SMALL STEPS, BIG MOMENTUM

We often underestimate what one focused step can do.

- One honest conversation you've been avoiding.
- One hour a day dedicated to building what's next.
- One weekly rhythm to rest and reset your mind.
- One decision to finally act on what you already know.

Momentum doesn't require perfection. It requires consistency.

When you move with focus, even in small ways, your life starts to send a different message to your mind: "We are not who we used to be. We move differently now." That internal agreement is how habits are formed, and habits are how legacies are built.

You've now seen all seven principles and the seven phases underneath them:

1. **Awareness** – You cannot heal what you hide.
2. **Ownership** – Your life is your responsibility.
3. **Identity** – Your norms become your narrative.
4. **Disempowering doubt** – Let your yes be yes.
5. **Vision** – Purpose over applause.
6. **Connection** – Alignment over access.
7. **Execution** – Focused action creates traction.

Becoming is the work.

You won't walk through these phases once and be done. You will cycle through them at every level of your life, each time at a deeper, more refined level. But now you have language and a framework for what that journey looks like.

Which phase do you feel you're standing in right now—and what is one focused step you're willing to take this week to honor it?

CHAPTER SEVEN

WHO DO I NEED TO BECOME?

VERY EARLY IN my journey, I fell into the trap of believing that I didn't have everything I needed to step fully into my calling of impacting lives.

I was a young man, already somewhat acclimated to the culture in the United States, yet feeling a deep sense of misalignment and unfulfillment in my postmission job. I had just acquired a position as a territory sales manager for a dental surgery company. My responsibility was to build relationships with different dentists in my community and act as a liaison between them and the surgery center, driving referrals to achieve quality care for pediatric patients.

Even as I write this now, I can see the nobility in a career like that. It made a real difference in people's lives, and I was genuinely excited to be a part of it. But that excitement, if I'm honest, was shortlived.

Because even though I knew I was helping people, I also felt misalignment and dissonance. I knew I wasn't helping in the way I was uniquely called to help.

Life can be so intricate and so dynamic. We can find ourselves doing something that is close to our calling, but not quite in it—doing good work, but not in the way we were uniquely and authentically created to do it. In that space, even when it's a noble venture, something in us knows we're off.

The job wasn't physically demanding, but it was emotionally draining. I wasn't tired because of the workload; I was tired because I felt like I was suppressing the fullness of what I carried. I was doing meaningful work, but not in the way that matched my design.

I still remember the day it broke. I was driving to a dentist's office, and after coming out of that appointment, I got back into my vehicle and let out one of the loudest screams of frustration I have ever released in my life.

It felt like I had this pentup purpose fighting to get out of me, and I kept rejecting it. I had no idea how I was supposed to impact lives by teaching, inspiring, sharing, challenging, and consulting when there were so many gaps between my desire to do it and my current ability to do it. Those gaps weren't just financial. Yes, I had experience in developing people, but I had never done so on my own at the scale I felt called to.

That scream was my soul saying, I'm tired of this feeling. I want more.

After the frustration subsided, a strange, overwhelming peace came over me—the kind of peace that often shows up when we finally get honest. In that peace, I heard a phrase that became a catalyst for the trajectory of my life:

"If you want to change your position, you must first change your perspective."

Those might sound like simple words, but I knew exactly what they meant. The change I was looking for was closer than I thought. To some degree, my path was already aligned.

It hit me: I was already meeting doctors. I was already building relationships with intelligent, powerful people who were struggling with building team culture—something I was not only gifted in but experienced in.

That realization became a bridge. I could see that I could fill the gap of helping medical professionals—people serving patients every single day—to be better served themselves. I could support them with strategies, tactics, and structures to build healthy teams so they could offer the best quality patient care.

In a quick moment, it all made sense. My perspective around my current position shifted. I stopped seeing where I was as an inconvenience to my purpose and started seeing it as a bridge into my purpose.

That shift empowered me. My days stopped feeling like a series of daunting tasks and started to feel like opportunities to gain insight, experience, and connection for my next.

I wish I could tell you that once I left that opportunity to pursue my purpose, everything flowed perfectly. It didn't.

I made a bold step to leave that career and step fully into my calling. I made the bold step with my actions—but not with my heart.

My actions were moving, but my heart was doubting.

My heart wasn't doubting because I didn't believe in the work. It was doubting because I didn't believe in my ability to do it at the highest level. I didn't believe I had everything I needed in order to do so.

One of the biggest things you hear when you're starting any kind of business or idea is, "You need capital." I won't diminish that. There is power in having the resources to walk into your next. Resources help you spread your reach and build with excellence and sustainability.

But my real struggle wasn't just that I lacked resources. My struggle was that I believed my lack of resources was the thing keeping me from the launching pad of success.

I had the big vision—but not the big bank account. I had a desire to build a lifechanging business and products to complement it—but not the capital to do it easily. So for a very long time, I felt stuck. Not because I had nothing, but because I misinterpreted what I had.

I remember developing a game plan for the year—how I was going to start my consulting business in the healthcare space, what I needed financially, and what milestones I had to hit. Then I opened my bank account and could almost hear it laughing at me: "What exactly are you planning with what's in here?"

In that moment, something in me knew I needed a different approach. I decided to do a simple exercise. Instead of asking, "What can I build with the money I don't have?" I asked, "How else can I grow this business, market this message, and build relationships with clients if the capital isn't there yet?"

Something shifted—first in my mind, then in my heart, and finally in my strategy. I realized the real power was not in my access to resources, but in my access to being resourceful.

When I looked back over my life, I realized resourcefulness was in my DNA. I came from an island where my mother and father built businesses from almost nothing. They sent their children to the United States for school with a currency that was worth about a third of the U.S. dollar. That meant they had to work three times as hard just to meet the needs of our education.

My parents had very little, but they were relentlessly resourceful.

In a moment, it clicked:

The secret to my success would never be found in how many resources I had.

It would be found in my willingness to become resourceful.

Let me go a bit deeper.

If you're reading this and you have a dream—a desire to start something, buy your first family home, retire your parents, or create something that matters—and you look at your life and realize what you have and what you want don't align, that tension itself can be a gift.

Because that gap forces you to move from simply seeking resources to intentionally becoming resourceful.

In nearly a decade of doing business, here's what I've learned:

- When you have resources, you have something you can lose.
- When you are resourceful, you have something that cannot be taken from you.

If you are truly resourceful, you can be placed in any situation, in any market, at any time, and you will find a way to identify opportunity and structure that opportunity in a way that serves you and others.

There is power in not having everything you think you need. Because when you don't have it, you're left with one powerful option— if you choose it: to become what you're looking for.

This chapter is my attempt to encapsulate the power of what it means to go to the next level by focusing not just on what you want to achieve, but on who you need to become to manage the magnitude of what you hope to achieve.

We spend a lot of time asking, "What do I want to achieve?"

We don't spend nearly enough time asking, "Who do I need to become to carry this without it breaking me?"

Because to get it and not sustain it is torment.
To get it and not sustain it is disempowering.
To get it and not sustain it is, in many ways, to never have had it at all.

So in this chapter, I want to focus you on what happens when you commit to becoming the person who can carry what you are called to. How becoming often precedes receiving.

When we wait to receive in order to become, we rarely receive. We're not in the posture to manage what we're asking for, or we can't even recognize it when it arrives. But when we focus on becoming first, we arrive ready.

So as we kick off this chapter and continue your journey of transformation, let me ask you:

Who do you need to become in order to manage the magnitude of what you want to achieve?

VISION, RESOURCES, AND THE TENSION THAT GROWS YOU

In my keynotes and transformational experiences—especially those centered on business and organizational growth—I always propose a simple argument:

There are two things that should always be in tension with each other: your vision and your resources.

Your vision should be shouting at your resources, telling them they need to grow up.

Your resources should be shouting at your vision, telling it to slow down.

If your vision and your resources are always in perfect agreement, your vision probably isn't big enough.

Becoming is not just the process of going through growth. Becoming is also the process of coming into agreement with your true identity and essence.

I firmly believe that our lifelong journey to fulfillment is really our lifelong journey to find ourselves—not the version of us built from titles, experiences, and perceptions, but the version we were actually created to be.

The gap between who you have been and who you were created to be can only be closed through becoming.

There's a phrase I heard once that hit me deeply:

"I didn't know that I was me."

Your vision usually shows up in glimpses. You see hints of what you could be, but it doesn't become real to you until you start moving toward it. That's why I say:

Clarity is often granted in a moment, but it is refined through movement.

Becoming is critical because it is the only way you fully step into alignment and agreement with who you really are. The man writing this book today—the man on stages, in boardrooms, in classrooms—I didn't know I was this person when I first saw the vision.

What it required was my submission to the process of becoming. Whether I submitted willingly or felt forced into it by divine circumstances, I still had to go through it.

Sometimes the vision arrives before the revelation of who you really are so that you have something to stretch toward. As you stretch, you become—and as you become, you finally see more clearly what you've been chasing.

At first, I thought it was all about consulting organizations and motivating people on stages. But as I kept leaning in, I realized something deeper. Through becoming, I discovered that I wasn't just a motivational speaker or consultant. I was an influencer of change. When I speak, when I design strategies, when I coach—that's all an extension of that core identity.

Becoming is the only way you discover who you really are.

COMPARISON, "READINESS," AND WHY YOU DON'T DICTATE THE TRAINING

Let me be vulnerable.

When I started my speaking career, I wrestled heavily with comparison. From the outside, if you know me, that might sound strange. People often assume I'm endlessly confident because of how I show up on stage. But my confidence doesn't come from ego; it comes from how deeply I care about the work.

Underneath that, I still had insecurity.

I compared myself to other speakers—their style, their stages, their impact. I would pace, practice, and feel this internal tension: I know I have what it takes to operate at that level. Why am I still in small rooms?

I remember saying over and over, "I'm ready. I'm so ready for bigger moments."

Looking back, that was distasteful. It was arrogant. It was ego dressed up as readiness.

Now that I am in bigger rooms—with a more refined version of myself—I understand something I couldn't see then. I thought I was ready, but I had no idea what it really takes to do this work at a high level.

Many of us get frustrated because we're not experiencing the moments we believe we're ready for. But here's what becoming has taught me:

You don't get to dictate the training when you don't understand the full extent of the game.

I grew up playing sports. Being from the Caribbean, one of those sports was cricket. If you don't understand cricket, I'm sorry—you're missing out on one of the greatest games ever.

One of my first coaches, the late Hayden Walsh, was one of the most influential people in my life. Every weekend, countless kids would come to his Technical Cricket Academy. We'd run drills, get coaching, and build community.

As kids, many of the drills didn't make sense. We ran through cones, made sharp pivots, repeated strange movements that, on the surface, just looked like a bunch of kids burning energy. But over time, I noticed my ball contact improved. My handeye coordination got sharper. My fundamentals grew stronger.

What looked random was actually deliberate. The drills were shaping us for a game we didn't yet understand.

Becoming often looks the same way.

You feel like you're being put through drills that don't make sense. You're running patterns you don't enjoy. You're being stretched in ways that feel unnecessary. But those very drills are developing what you will need to manage the magnitude of the "game" you haven't fully seen yet.

These days, I'm learning not to complain to the Coach—God—about the process or the development. I don't fully understand the level He's preparing me for.

You might be frustrated because you think you're ready for the level you can see. But what if you're actually being prepared for a level much greater than you can currently imagine? Resisting the process of becoming might be shrinking the scale of what you're capable of impacting.

Again: you don't get to dictate the training when you don't know the full extent of the game.

EMBODIMENT: YOU CAN'T GIVE WHAT YOU DON'T HAVE

If I were to summarize becoming in one big thought, it would be this:

Becoming is about fully embodying what your calling represents.

Embodiment matters because it gives you the substance you need for authentic impact.

Imagine we're sitting at a dinner table and I ask you to pass the salt. Your first instinct will not be to lecture me about salt. You wouldn't "brand" salt, perform salt, or post salt. You would reach for it, take hold of it, and then give it.

You can only give it because you first have it in your hands.

In a world driven by what looks good instead of what is good, many people are more committed to the appearance of having something than *actually* possessing it.

Becoming is the process that ensures that when the spotlight hits you, it's hitting someone who truly carries what they claim to carry.

Because you cannot give sustainably what you do not have intrinsically.

So here's an exercise for your becoming journey:

- Write down the impact you want to make in this world—the business, the idea, the leadership, the way you want to show up for your family, team, or community.
- Then ask yourself: Who do I need to become to embody this?

When you focus on embodiment, your life starts to overflow. You stop performing impact and start being the kind of person whose very presence creates it.

What you want to give others becomes the blueprint for who you need to become.

As I wrap this chapter, I'm reminded of a story about a young boy and his grandfather.

They were standing outside near a massive boulder. The grandfather asked, "My son, what do you want to accomplish with your life?"

The boy replied, "I want to be wildly successful. I want to be fulfilled in every area. I want to do work that matters. I want to add value—and I want to be valued for the value I add."

The grandfather smiled. "Are you sure that's really what you want?"

"Yes, Granddad. More than anything."

"Then I'm going to give you the secret," he said. "If you truly want that level of success and fulfillment, go over there and push that rock."

The boy smirked, confused, but trusted his grandfather. He walked over and started pushing.

At first, he pushed with desire—full of passion, zeal, and excitement about all the possibilities.

But the rock didn't move. So he did what most of us do. He pushed harder.

Still, nothing.

Days turned into weeks. Weeks into months. Months into years. His passion turned into frustration, then into duty. He kept showing up, pushing, but his heart wasn't in it anymore. He saw no movement, so he assumed there was no purpose.

Finally, he came back to his grandfather exhausted and defeated. "Granddad, I've been pushing this rock for years. Every morning I show up, and it never moves. I told you I wanted to be successful and add value. But this isn't working."

The grandfather smiled gently. "If you trust me, go push it one more time."

The boy sighed, but obeyed. He walked back to the rock and began to push again. Tears ran down his face. Sweat rolled down his brow. At one point he lifted a hand to wipe his forehead—and froze.

His hands were bigger.

His arms were stronger.

His chest, his back, his legs—all had grown.

He ran back to his grandfather, stunned. "Granddad! The rock didn't move—but I did. Look at me. I'm stronger now than I've ever been."

His grandfather smiled and said, "Now you understand. The purpose of the rock was never to move. The purpose of the rock was to move something inside of you—to make you strong enough to handle what's on the other side of it."

Then he handed his grandson a small packed bag and said, "Now you're ready to face every obstacle the world will send you in pursuit of your success. Not just because you walked the journey—but because you chose to push the rock."

Many times, the journey of becoming looks like pushing a rock that won't move. You push a dream, a relationship, a business, a calling—and for a long time, it looks like nothing is happening.

But what if the point was never the rock?
What if the point was your development?

What if the adversity, the delay, the lack of obvious resources, the resistance—was all designed to give you stronger arms, a stronger back, stronger legs, and a stronger heart?

Maybe for you, the rock is helping you move from judgment to curiosity, from criticism to love, from scarcity to abundance.

For me, one of the greatest shifts was moving from the prison of believing I was stuck because of a lack of resources to the freedom of knowing I am powerful because I am resourceful.

Because in the end, true success is not just about what you accomplish.

It is about who you become in the process.

CHAPTER EIGHT

UNSHAKABLE CONFIDENCE

THERE IS A kind of power that has nothing to do with titles, bank accounts, or how loud your voice is in a room, yet when you encounter it, you can feel it before a word is even spoken. It is the power to create, to become, to restore, to forgive, to love, to impact, and to heal, and the more I have watched people, coached leaders, and navigated my own journey, the more convinced I am that every one of us is already standing in proximity to that power. We either learn how to harness it, or we remain one decision away from it.

The power I am talking about in this chapter is what I call unshakable confidence. Not the kind of "confidence" that is really insecurity dressed in designer clothes, not the type that needs to be the loudest voice in the room, dominate every conversation, and bulldoze others just to feel significant, but a deeper confidence that is rooted in authenticity, anchored in truth, and expressed in a quiet strength that does not need to announce itself to be felt. This kind of confidence is not performative; it is possessed.

You have probably met both versions. There is the version of "confidence" that shows up as arrogance, the person who walks into a room and immediately starts posturing, talking over people, flexing their résumé or their possessions, trying to convince everyone that they belong there, when in reality much of what they are doing is attempting to cover a gnawing feeling of inadequacy with the blanket of ego. Their volume is not evidence of power; it is evidence of panic.

Then there is another kind of presence altogether. This is the person who can enter a space without saying much at all, yet something about their posture, their poise, and their peace commands attention. People lean in, not because this individual is demanding it, but because there is a settledness about them that feels different in a world addicted to pretending. Their very being communicates, "I know who I am, I know what I carry, and I do not have to compete with you to express it." That is the kind of confidence I want to talk about.

In this chapter, I want to pull confidence down from the clouds of hype and bring it into the practical, everyday places of your life. I am not going to give you a sevenstep motivational checklist that evaporates the moment pressure shows up. Instead, I want to walk you through three core principles that form the foundation of unshakable confidence. They are deceptively simple, which is why many people overlook them in search of something more glamorous, but in my experience these three are the difference between confidence that crumbles and confidence that endures: gratitude, humility, and forgiveness.

These are not random character traits; they are deliberate practices that determine how much unnecessary weight your soul is carrying at any given moment. And that matters, because the more weight you carry that you were never meant to hold, the harder it is to walk in the power you actually possess. Power, in its truest form, is not about how much you can stack on your shoulders; it is about how freely and fully you can move through life because you have learned to release what does not belong to you.

Let's start with the first pillar.

GRATITUDE: MOVING FROM FEELING TO FOCUS

Most of us were taught, directly or indirectly, that gratitude is a feeling. If life is going well—if the deal closes, if the relationship is thriving, if the bank account looks healthy—then we say we "feel grateful." If not, gratitude feels out of reach, almost dishonest.

I have come to see gratitude very differently. Gratitude, at its core, is not a feeling; gratitude is a focus. It is not just an emotion that visits you when conditions are right; it is a deliberate lens you choose to look through, especially when conditions are not.

When gratitude is only a feeling, you celebrate when life gives you what you want. When gratitude becomes a focus, you recognize that the greatest gift is life itself. You no longer wait for perfect circumstances to say "thank you"; you begin from the reality that every breath is evidence that possibility still exists.

That shift sounds poetic until you are sitting in the middle of a hard season. Maybe you are in an apartment where the rent is overdue and the notices are piling up. Maybe you are at your desk, wondering how you are going to meet payroll for the people who trust you. Maybe you are lying in a bed you once shared with someone who is no longer there, the silence reminding you of what you have lost. In those moments, the idea of gratitude can feel almost offensive.

So let me offer you something simple and tangible.

Take your right hand and place it over your chest.

If you feel that steady rhythm beneath your palm, I want you to understand that what you are feeling is not just a heartbeat; it is a reminder that possibility is still possible. That heartbeat is evidence that you are not finished yet, that there are still chapters of your story waiting to be written, that there is still something in you that the world has not fully seen. That alone is something to be grateful for.

We live in a culture that tells us power shows up first as money, status, and external success. But money does not lead; it follows. It follows value, integrity, consistency, persistence, effort, and discipline. It follows a life that is aligned and a heart that is willing to keep showing up. None of those things can even be expressed without life. So when you practice gratitude for life itself, you are not settling; you are aligning with the very foundation that everything else is built on.

Gratitude does not mean you pretend everything is okay. It means that even when everything is not okay, you refuse to let what is missing blind you to what remains. It is the discipline of asking, "What is still here? What is still working? What can I still build from?" And that discipline changes you, because you stop moving from desperation and start moving from sufficiency.

The opposite of gratitude is not simply complaining; the opposite of gratitude is entitlement. Entitlement is the posture that says, "Everything, like the sun, should revolve around me. Life owes me." When you live entitled, you will never experience deep peace, because nothing will ever feel like enough. There will always be another person to compare yourself to, another milestone to chase, another reason to feel behind.

Gratitude breaks that cycle. When you practice gratitude as a focus, you magnify what is real and enduring, and you minimize what is loud but fleeting. You begin to see clearly: I may not have everything I desire yet, but I have enough to start. I may not be where I thought I would be, but I am not where I used to be. I may be carrying grief, but I am also carrying grace. That perspective is not just positive thinking; it is the soil in which unshakable confidence grows.

HUMILITY: DYING TO SELF WITHOUT KILLING YOUR WORTH

If gratitude resets your focus, humility resets your motive.

Humility is another word that has been mishandled. Many people hear "humility" and picture someone shrinking back, downplaying their gifts, refusing to own their value, or constantly talking about how unworthy they are. That is not humility; that is insecurity with a softer tone.

True humility does not deny your worth. It acknowledges that your worth does not make you the center of the universe.

The way I define humility is this: **humility is the relentless pursuit of dying to self.**

Not dying to your identity, not dying to your calling, but dying to the need to make everything about you—your comfort, your convenience, your image, your gain.

We live in a "selflove" culture, and while healthy selflove matters deeply, what often gets labeled as selflove is actually selfabsorption. It becomes all about what I can get, what I can accumulate, how I can be seen, how I can benefit. When that becomes the center of your life, you unintentionally create a version of yourself that is constantly hungry and never satisfied, because you have built your sense of significance on how much you can extract from every situation.

Humility invites you into a different posture.

It shifts your first question from "What can I get out of this?" to "What can I give to this? How can I show up here in a way that brings value? How can I serve?" That shift is not about erasing yourself; it is about rightly ordering yourself. You still matter, but you are no longer the only one who does.

I often say that calling dies in comfort, contribution dies in comfort, and vision dies in comfort. When the highest goal of your life is to feel comfortable, you will avoid the very experiences that are designed to expand you. You will say no to the opportunities that stretch you. You will resist the conversations that refine you. You will stay where it is safe, and in doing so you will slowly suffocate the very calling you keep saying you want to fulfill.

Humility does not mean you never rest or that you burn yourself out to prove a point. It means you are willing to step beyond what is convenient when obedience, purpose, or love require it. It means you choose to live for something bigger than your own comfort.

And here is the paradox: the more you live for something beyond yourself, the more grounded and confident you become. When your sense of worth is tied only to your own comfort, your confidence will crumble every time life disrupts that comfort. But when your confidence is tied to your character, your contribution, and your alignment with your assignment, it becomes much harder to shake.

Humility also protects the people around you. You can be gifted, talented, and influential and still be safe to be around when humility is present, because you are not using your gift to build an empire of ego; you are using it to build people. You understand that what you carry is not meant to be hoarded; it is meant to be poured out in a way that honors God, honors others, and honors the person you are becoming.

In this way, humility does not diminish your power. It directs it. It keeps your confidence from becoming a weapon and turns it into a covering instead.

FORGIVENESS: RELEASING WHAT WAS NEVER MEANT TO BE CARRIED

If gratitude lightens your perspective and humility lightens your motives, forgiveness lightens your heart.

Forgiveness is one of the most misunderstood components of unshakable confidence. Many of us think forgiveness is primarily about the other person—that if we forgive, it means we are saying what they did was okay, or that the pain didn't matter, or that justice is no longer important. That is not forgiveness; that is denial.

Forgiveness, as I see it, is not the justification of what happened; it is your refusal to keep carrying the weight of it. Forgiveness is the decision to say, "I will not allow this event, this betrayal, this disappointment—whether it was done to me or by me—to dictate the rest of my life."

We often believe that holding on to our hurt, our anger, or our desire for payback gives us some kind of power. We tell ourselves, "If I let this go, they win. If I forgive, it means they got away with it." So we grip the wound with both hands, rehearsing the story over and over, convinced that our refusal to release it is a form of control.

But here is the truth: ***what you hold on to will eventually turn on you and begin to hold on to you.***

Unforgiveness is like putting a brick in your backpack every time you relive the offense. At first, the weight feels manageable. In fact, sometimes you slam that brick into the bag with pride, thinking, "I'll show them. I'll carry this and let it fuel me." But as time passes and more bricks are added—resentment, bitterness, cynicism, selfprotection—that backpack becomes heavier. The very thing you thought was giving you strength is actually draining it.

Every brick you add reduces your capacity to carry the weight of what actually matters: your calling, your relationships, your creativity, your leadership, your joy. You find yourself exhausted, not just physically, but emotionally and spiritually. Confidence becomes harder and harder to access, not because you lack power, but because you are too weighed down to walk in it.

Forgiveness is not a feeling. Forgiveness is a choice you may have to make more than once—a choice to release the debt, to stop rehearsing the story in a way that keeps you locked in the role of the victim, and to reclaim your energy for what you are called to build.

Sometimes the hardest person to forgive is not someone else; it is yourself. Many of us are imprisoned by our own perfectionism and regret. We replay decisions we wish we had made differently, seasons where we felt like we failed, moments where we hurt others or ourselves, and we allow those snapshots to become our permanent identity. Forgiving yourself does not mean pretending it didn't happen;

it means acknowledging it, learning from it, and then refusing to let that version of you be the only version you ever become.

Forgiveness says, "I may not be able to change the past, but I will not let the past continue to change me in ways that keep me from my future."

POWER AS A WEIGHTLESS WALK

When you weave these three principles together—gratitude, humility, and forgiveness—something powerful begins to happen.

Gratitude helps you release the weight of entitlement, the belief that life owes you something and that you cannot be at peace until you have it. Humility helps you release the weight of ego, the constant need to center yourself, to prove yourself, to make everything about your gain. Forgiveness helps you release the weight of offense, disappointment, and regret that you have been carrying like bricks in your own backpack.

As those weights begin to drop, your posture changes. You stand a little taller, not because you have acquired more external trophies, but because you are no longer hunched over internally. Your walk becomes lighter, not because life suddenly became easy, but because you are only carrying what belongs to you.

This is why I say that *power is the result of a weightless walk*. Real power is not about adding more armor, more pretense, more performance. It is about shedding everything that keeps you from moving freely in who you already are and who you are becoming.

When you are not practicing gratitude, when you refuse humility, when you resist forgiveness, you are loading yourself down every single day. And then you wonder why you feel tired, why your confidence feels inconsistent, why the smallest setback shakes you. It is not that you are weak; it is that you are weighed down.

Unshakable confidence is not something you put on like an outfit; it is something you uncover as you remove what never belonged to you in the first place.

THE PARADOX OF POWER

There is a paradox when it comes to power and confidence that I want you to understand: you can have power and still not always feel powerful.

There will be days when doubt creeps in, when fear whispers louder than faith, when your circumstances do not look like your confession. Unshakable confidence does not mean you never feel those things. It means that even when you do, you remember that power is still accessible. You remember that at any given moment you can choose gratitude over entitlement, humility over ego, and forgiveness over bitterness—and in doing so, you can begin to ignite what has been dormant inside you.

On the other side of that kind of ownership is power. Not the kind that depends on likes, titles, or applause, but the kind that flows from a mind that has been renewed, a heart that has been softened, and hands that are willing to build.

If your mind can conceive this, and your heart is willing to believe it, then your hands can begin to create a life, a legacy, and a level of impact that reflect who you are becoming, not who you used to be. That is unshakable confidence.

And as you cultivate it, remember this: everything we are doing in this part of the journey is about identity. It is about becoming the kind of person who can carry what you are asking for. Confidence is not a separate accessory you add to your life; it is the natural byproduct of walking in alignment with who you truly are.

PART THREE

TRANSFORM YOUR LIFE

BORROWED DREAMS, BROKEN METRICS

Most people are running full steam toward
a destination that, once they arrive, they
will recognize was never for them.

I FIRMLY BELIEVE in the power of living a fulfilled life. If you were to ask me, "Jovan, what is your goal in life?" I would tell you that my goal is to live a life where I authentically fulfill the purpose that God created me to fulfill, in the way I was uniquely created to do so—to be the husband, father, business partner, leader, philanthropist, and all of the other titles that flow out of who I was created to be, not in place of it.

I want you to sit with me in this chapter, because I believe this is going to be one of the most challenging chapters for many people to walk through, and honestly, it is challenging for me to write. Not because I lack belief in the magnitude of what I am about to share, but because this is one of the most overlooked and undervalued aspects of life. We live in a world, shaped by people's perceptions, by cultural narratives, and even by certain interpretations of "success," that constantly fights against this notion of fulfillment and purpose. We glorify success and quietly diminish fulfillment.

I want to suggest that success and fulfillment are not necessarily the same thing.

Here is how I see it. Success, in my opinion, is the accomplishment of a thing—the achievement of a position, a possession, or a level of prominence. It is usually connected to something tangible. Success is the promotion to the corner office, the beautiful house on several acres of land, the brandnew luxury vehicle, the zeros at the end of a number in a bank account, the trophy on the shelf. These things can validate, at least temporarily, that there is some level of worth or recognition attached to our lives.

Fulfillment, on the other hand, is different. Fulfillment is not just the achievement of getting something; it is the achievement of becoming something. It usually shows up in the space of joy, peace, contentment, love, embrace—a quiet knowing that who you are and how you are living are in agreement. Fulfillment lives in the realm of what is not always easy to measure, but it is, in reality, the very reason most of us pursue success in the first place. We don't chase the thing only because of the thing; we chase the thing because of how we hope it will make us feel and who we hope it will allow us to become.

So in a sense, we pursue what we *want* (success) in order to ultimately achieve what we *need* (fulfillment).

Let me be very clear: I am not against things. I am not against nice things, or working hard, or achieving a level of success that allows you to have experiences, comfort, or even luxury. I believe life is meant to be enjoyed. What I am really after in this chapter is the way we prioritize the pursuit. I am after the reality that many of us are prioritizing success, hoping it will lead us to fulfillment, when in truth the order should be reversed.

What I have found is that the true pursuit of our lives should be the pursuit of fulfillment, and by doing so, we allow the things we used to chase to begin to chase us. I believe that what you chase will always run from you, but what you *pursue*—from the right place—will eventually find you. There is a difference. We can spend so much of our lives chasing versus pursuing.

Here is another way to say it: when you chase things from a place of emptiness, even if you catch them, there will always be a "better" thing, a bigger thing, a nicer thing, a faster thing, a wealthier thing. The road of chasing is endless and exhausting, because the finish line keeps moving. But when you begin to pursue fulfillment—when you live from identity, authenticity, and calling—everything you would have chased now has to chase you. And here is the shift: it chases a version of you that does not need to be validated by it.

Can I go a bit deeper?

Chasing is usually what we do when we go after things out of a void, hoping that the thing will fill a place in us that allows us to finally feel valuable. Pursuing, on the other hand, is what we do when we move toward something from value—from identity, from authenticity, from love. When you pursue from value, the car, the house, the account, the title—none of it can ultimately define you. And if it cannot define you, it cannot derail you. I want you to slow down and read that again: *if it cannot define you, it will never derail you.*

In my own life, and in working with individuals who have a high level of success but are not fulfilled, I have seen how much of their peace, power, presence, and poise is directly connected to things. So when the things go, so do they. But on the other hand, individuals who have a high level of fulfillment *and* success are not dictated by the rise and fall of what they have, because they understand that their inherent value is rooted in a life that has been centered around pursuing fulfillment, not chasing validation.

So before we go any further, I want to ask you a question:

Are you only chasing success, or are you pursuing fulfillment and allowing success to chase you?

How do you know? What does that actually look like? And why does it matter?

This chapter—Borrowed Dreams and Broken Metrics—is not just another chapter to read; I believe it has the potential to become one of the defining moments that refines and redefines what you pursue. Because maybe the very essence of your transformation is not primarily found in your work ethic, but in your motive. Not so much in *what* you are doing, but in the *place* you are doing it from and the *reason* you are doing it for.

In many of the earlier chapters, we did what I would call brain surgery—examining thought patterns, beliefs, and internal narratives. This chapter is about heart surgery. That is why it may feel uncomfortable. But if you are willing to stay on the table, I believe it can change the way you measure everything.

You ready? Let's go.

CREATED ON PURPOSE, FOR A PURPOSE

Everything about the work that I do stems from a foundational principle and a truth I choose to build my life on: *we were all created on purpose for a purpose.* I am not one of those believers who thinks that life is accidental, that we're just here because a random cosmic explosion happened, a meteor hit the planet, monkeys evolved, and eventually we showed up with no intention behind any of it. That is not my belief. I believe this is far greater than that.

I believe our very existence is something that, even if we tried, we could not fully understand in this life—not at the magnitude we attempt to. I believe we were created by a Creator. I believe this was all designed, that there was a destiny predesigned for our lives. I'll share more about the depths of my personal beliefs in an upcoming book, but I've seen too much, experienced too much, and the evidence of my own life has shown me constantly that there is a purpose in all of this, and ultimately what we choose to do with our time matters.

You may have heard people say the two most important days in your life are the day you are born and the day you find out why. I love that. I also think about the tombstone that represents the end of our earthly life: your name, your starting date, your end date, and that small dash in the middle. I've heard it said—and I agree—that what you do with that dash is what truly matters.

I would add this: when your name comes up in conversation, what people think about, and the evidence they can point to from your life, is the essence of whether that dash was lived well. Because our lives, when you strip everything else away, are really defined by one word: impact.

You'll never see a UHaul behind a hearse, as Denzel Washington often says. So many thought leaders talk about the fact that you can't take things with you. Much of what we pursue—excuse me, what we chase—in this life cannot come with us when we leave. When we evaluate a life, the only thing that really matters is that word: impact.

How did my life impact the people I came into contact with, and what is the ripple effect of that impact? That is what drives me, and in my conviction, that is what should ultimately drive each of us while we still have breath in our lungs and a heart beating in our chest.

So on a daytoday basis, the question becomes:

- What impact am I making?
- What impact am I making in my home, with my family, with my kids?
- What impact do I make in the classroom, the boardroom, the community, the job, the spaces I frequent?

When we celebrated my father's life, nobody stood up and talked about the clothes he wore, the cars he drove, or the house we lived in. People gathered to celebrate his life because of the impact he made in theirs.

I want you to pause here and consider this question: What impact will you make with your life? And as you answer that question, can you point back to specific, intentional actions you are taking every single day that align with that impact? Are you waiting for something to happen to you, or are you stepping into the authority, identity, power, and purpose you've been given and allowing life to happen through you—for the sake of others?

Impact matters.

TIME, IMPACT, AND THE WEIGHT OF ALIGNMENT

If we accept that each of us has a unique purpose—and that purpose is expressed through how we live our lives to impact the life of another—then we also have to accept that what we do with our time matters. Time is a limited resource. We are not making more of it. How we use it ultimately determines the quality of our lives and the magnitude of our impact.

Every day when we get up, where we go and what we pursue carry a lingering question on the other side: What impact am I making? And, even deeper—the premise of this chapter—Am I making the impact I was uniquely created and assigned to make, or am I making an impact that is convenient, comfortable, or simply aligned with how people perceive me?

I want to take my time here, because I think it is critical. We have to cautiously and intentionally evaluate our lives to ensure we are living from a place of authenticity and alignment, not from a place of conformity. One of the most helpful ways I've found to see this clearly is to describe what it actually feels like when we are not living in alignment—when we are living what I call a life of borrowed dreams and broken metrics.

In my experience, three things often show up:

1.   No Passion
2.   No Focus
3.   No Fun

SYMPTOM ONE: NO PASSION

The first sign is that you move through your days with no passion, no fire, no real enthusiasm for your life. It feels like you're on autopilot—going through the motions, doing what is expected of you. You might do it well because you have the head for it, but your heart is missing.

In this life you need both. Head organizes priorities. Heart provides passion. Passion is only sustainably ignited when you are operating from alignment. It's the energy that allows you to bring your full self to the work, not just your skill set.

So when you find yourself in extended seasons where there is no passion, no fire, no sense of aliveness in the work you do, it may be an indication that you could be out of alignment with your assignment.

SYMPTOM TWO: NO FOCUS

The second sign is a specific kind of lack of focus. I am not talking here about medical or biological realities that can affect concentration—those are real, and I don't minimize them. I'm talking about a different kind of focus: *an internal conviction to commit to the work necessary for your purpose to be revealed.*

This level of focus has less to do with your ability to sit still and more to do with your willingness to enter the quiet spaces of preparation. It is the focus that gets you into the study, the reading, the practice, the learning, the coaching, the designing, the refining of solutions—without needing someone else to constantly light a fire under you.

It's the thing you do without someone having to hold you accountable, because you feel an internal pull toward the vision. You know you are responsible for bringing something to life. Purpose is a pulling force—it pulls you in the direction of your destiny, and you don't need a standing ovation to respond.

This is the kind of focus that separates those who are simply pursuing a position from those who are pursuing purpose. If you continually struggle to lock in when nobody is watching, if you only move when someone else is pushing you, if you cannot seem to become your own compass and standard, that lack of focus may be a sign that you are pursuing something that looks good to you but may not actually be made for you.

SYMPTOM THREE: NO FUN

The third sign is tricky because "fun" can sound trivial, but I would argue that when something you're doing never feels like fun—when you don't enjoy it, don't love it, and it never awakens your childlike wonder—that's worth paying attention to.

As we grow into adulthood and accumulate failures, setbacks, and responsibilities, we often bury or suppress the parts of us that used to dream freely. But when you are walking in alignment, there is usually at least some space where that childlike curiosity resurfaces. You find yourself thinking about what is possible, about what this could become, and you bring a level of creativity and ingenuity to the work.

When all of that disappears—when you have become rigid, stoic, and you are doing it purely out of duty and not out of any real desire—that can be another indication of misalignment with your assignment.

I want you to consider your own daytoday life. Do you recognize yourself in any of these frames—not just on a bad day or a rough week, but in extended seasons? Seasons where:

- You lack passion and fire.
- You lack the internal focus to prepare in private for what you are called to do in public.
- You have lost the sense of joy, curiosity, and creative engagement.

If so, it may be a sign that you have compromised your purpose in order to chase a position.

WHAT IS A BORROWED DREAM?

A borrowed dream, in its essence, is a deliberate decision—whether conscious or not—to settle for what serves your position at the cost of rising to what serves your purpose. It is when we accept someone else's definition of success or someone else's assignment as our own, for a variety of reasons.

Borrowed dreams show up when we:

- Accept roles or paths simply because they are applauded or expected.
- Confuse other people's comfort or approval with confirmation of our calling.
- Try to cram misalignment into our lives and label it authenticity.

It is where we reject the premise that we have a unique purpose and assignment, and instead act as if none of this really matters, as if whatever we do will have the same weight and impact. It is when we are running full steam toward a destination that was never meant for us, playing for a championship in a game we were never meant to compete in.

I am passionate about borrowed dreams not just because they cost us our fulfillment, but because of the ripple effect they have when we operate outside of alignment with our unique calling, gifts, and purpose.

Do you realize that someone's purpose tomorrow is contingent on your purpose today? That what happens with the generation coming after us is directly connected to how we respond to our assignment now? Life, especially from generation to generation, is like a 4x100 relay. Each generation runs their leg and then passes the baton to the next. How you pass the baton matters.

If we pass a baton that is disconnected from what the next generation needs, we create a gap—not because we didn't exist, but because we chose to exist instead of truly live.

You may never know that your purpose as a paramedic today is to rush a child to the hospital who needs to see the doctor that helps them recover, and that child is destined to become the next president. You may not realize that your purpose as a teacher is to empower the student who will one day discover a cure for a disease. You may never see that your leadership in your company positions it to serve customers whose lives are changed in ways you will never hear about.

Impact is powerful because it always reaches farther than your awareness. You will impact people you will never meet. That is the magnitude of purpose—it creates a ripple effect that allows the next generation to continue and expand the assignment.

My concern is this: we live in a time where many are willing to accept borrowed dreams for three main reasons—

1. Limited by identity.
2. Crippled by validation.
3. Deceived by comfort.

LIMITED BY IDENTITY

Lack of identity is at the root of so much of our ability to achieve, to succeed, to live, and to love, because all of those are directly connected to identity—knowing who we are. To know who you are is also to know who you are not. To know who you are is to know how you should show up in certain situations, to know your gifts and abilities, to know what you value. All of these premises are instrumental not just to purpose but to your quantifiable value in the world and in the marketplace.

When we don't know who we are, we end up accepting anything and defining ourselves around whatever we choose to accept. We define ourselves around titles, around the roles we play, around all of the different pieces. To some degree, we even find our identity in what we do.

There is a powerful concept that really empowered me in my own life and I believe would be a significant shift for most people if we truly understood it: you are not what you do, but who you are determines how well you do what you do. I want you to read that again. So many of us wrap our identity up in our work and in our titles.

What happens then is that when those things are not going in a great direction, or when we experience challenges or adversity, we start to believe we are those things. We can never truly shift unless the thing is happening exactly the way we expect or want it to happen. But when your identity is different from the reality of your title, if you have a bad week, a bad month, a bad sales performance, or a bad business year, those things do not define you—you ultimately define them. You are able to reestablish your results, your title, your wins as a representative of who you are, instead of allowing them to define who you are.

Here's the tension: when we lack identity, we are constantly looking for other things to validate who we are, and we end up taking on what looks good on others in order to find ourselves in that thing.

The journey of discovering your identity is so critical because it's not until you do that you can truly discern and decipher whether the dream you are going after is really for you, or if it just looks good on you.

What if this shift—either clarifying whether you're going after a borrowed dream, or refining the fact that you are actually on your current path—is directly connected to a continued, relentless quest of discovering who you are, not who you have been labeled to be?

CRIPPLED BY VALIDATION

One of the other kryptonites to stepping into alignment, instead of settling for a borrowed dream, is validation. For many of us, the borrowed dream—the version of ourselves built around position rather than actual purpose—comes with a level of validation that tells us we're "good enough," or even more dangerously, that we are enough because of it.

This is where most of us choose to camp. We pitch a tent and settle in the place where others have validated us, and we begin to form ourselves into what others have accepted. I dealt with this for a long time and didn't recognize it as a limitation until I had a significant shift in my life.

If you've followed my journey from the beginning—or even if I'm new to you—you may know that I started as a motivational speaker. I want to be clear: I have no issue with motivational speakers. I believe in the power of motivation. We all need encouragement, and I deeply respect anyone who dedicates their life to encouraging others.

But my story went a little differently. I started as a motivational speaker because that's what people perceived me to be when they heard me speak—and quite frankly, it was what the market was willing to pay me for. So I branded myself as a motivational speaker. Within my first year of business, I closed a lot of speaking opportunities. People were excited to book me in that lane, and I showed up and did just that—I motivated.

Yet, even as I fired people up, I always knew inside that I lacked the fulfillment I was searching for. In hindsight, that lack of fulfillment was an indication that I was operating out of position, not out of purpose.

The interesting part is that I was getting paid well. The easy thing would have been to keep building my brand around that. Stage after stage, standing ovation after standing ovation, I leaned into the motivational space. But I remember one particular event: West Coast, firstclass flight, private driver, the works. I walked off that stage to a standing ovation—and felt empty.

At first, I thought I was ungrateful. But in a moment of honest reflection, I realized my true metric of success was not just audience validation. It was whether people were taking the principles I was teaching, applying them in real time, and seeing transformational results in their lives and businesses. The emptiness I felt was because I wasn't sure that real change was happening beyond the moment.

Motivation had become a vehicle that paid me, but it also limited me. It kept me from stepping fully into who I really was. That's when I began talking about what I call *perception prison*.

Perception prison is the place people put you based on their perception. In my space, as a chocolate brother who communicates with conviction, power, and passion, the default categories are often preacher or hypeman motivational speaker, usually tied to church or sports. It hasn't historically been the norm for people to see someone who looks like me as a strategist, a systems thinker, a partner to executives and organizations on performance and transformation at scale.

Because people didn't know where to place me, they put me in the boxes they were familiar with. I'm not angry about that. Human beings categorize to survive; our brains need context, and context is always shaped by our experiences. So being put in perception prison is not the problem.

The problem starts when you begin to decorate the prison like it's your home.

That's what I did. I decorated that perceptual cell called "motivational speaker." My lack of fulfillment wasn't a lack of gratitude. It was a signal that I was limiting my abilities to what the market validated instead of what my purpose required.

In reality, I am not just a motivational speaker. I am an influencer of change. Motivation is what you may feel when you hear me, but it is not the totality of who I am.

So let me ask you: Have you become what other people have perceived you to be at the cost of becoming who you were created to be in purpose? That is perception prison. That is what happens when validation cripples you into settling for a borrowed dream instead of accepting the weight and wonder of your inherent purpose.

I don't discredit my journey, and I don't diminish the title, but I always knew there was more. It is nobody else's responsibility to step into that more for me. It is my responsibility to say no to a borrowed dream and yes to alignment with my assignment—which is my inherent purpose.

DECEIVED BY COMFORT

The final reason we often settle for borrowed dreams is because borrowed dreams are usually comfortable. Even though they may cost us something, they don't cost us the thing that is most difficult to sacrifice: our will and our way.

The kryptonite of our calling is our comfort. Comfort is primarily about protecting ourselves—protecting what makes sense to us, what feels safe, what doesn't stretch us. If we aren't careful, a life built around protecting ourselves can ultimately hinder us from a life of purpose.

A borrowed dream is comfortable because you can get by without fully applying yourself. It doesn't demand the highest levels of grit, stretching, seeking, and surrender that real impact requires. Most of us don't consciously want to be comfortable; we simply acquiesce to comfort because we've been through enough pain, failure, and adversity that we now resist anything that even resembles those seasons.

I've often said that sometimes your breakthrough will look a lot like the thing that almost broke you. I'm not advocating being reckless with your time, health, or wellbeing. I am saying that sometimes the thing you failed at in one season may require you to face it again with courage in another.

It might look like this:

- You failed at a business once, and now you've decided entrepreneurship "isn't for you," when in reality the first failure taught you what you needed to build the second one correctly.
- You went for a promotion and got denied, and concluded there are no growth opportunities for you in that company, when that denial might be protection or redirection toward a betterfitting role or a season of development.
- You walked through a painful divorce and now reject the idea of love or partnership altogether, when the love you truly desire may be found in the next relationship you allow yourself to consider.

Rejection can be protection. Rejection can be redirection. Either way, those experiences can be invitations for growth, evolution, and becoming.

Operating in discomfort doesn't simply mean "it's hard." It often just means "it's unfamiliar." What feels hard today, if you commit to working through it, can become normal tomorrow. The circumstances around your pursuit may not get easier; in many cases, they become more complex. But you develop greater capacity to handle them.

To submit your life to comfort is to gradually diminish your assignment, your purpose, and your calling.

ALIGNMENT METRICS: DEFINING WHAT SUCCESS REALLY MEANS TO YOU

When you begin the journey of discovering who you are and saying yes to the inherent purpose you were created to live—a purpose often revealed through the problems around you—you eventually have to address how you are measuring your life.

I don't believe we "find" purpose the way we find a lost wallet, because to find something you usually need to know what it looks like. Many people say they are searching for purpose without any sense of what they're actually looking for, so they wouldn't recognize it if they saw it. I believe we are invited to create purpose by how we bring our gifts to opportunities that align with what we value.

Here is a simple formula:

Gifts and abilities + opportunities that align with what you value = created purpose.

Your lifelong work becomes:

- Identifying and developing your gifts and abilities.
- Getting honest about what you truly value.
- Saying yes to, or creating, opportunities that align with those values.

Where these three intersect, purpose is created and expressed.

But to live this way, you need what I call alignment metrics—personal measurements of success rooted in your values, not in borrowed expectations.

If you never clarify what you value, you will default to chasing what everyone else celebrates. But when you name your values, those values become the ruler by which you measure your days.

Let me make this practical. Imagine someone whose core values include:

- **Family**: Being present, emotionally available, and creating memories together.
- **Freedom**: Having control over their time and the ability to make choices without being owned by debt or schedule.
- **Contribution**: Using their gifts to genuinely help people grow or heal.
- **Faith**: Living in a way that aligns with their convictions and honors God.

For that person, success can no longer be defined only as "more money" or "higher title." Their metrics must now sound like:

- Did I show up for my family in a way that reflects their importance to me?
- Do my financial and career decisions move me toward greater freedom or deeper bondage?
- Did I contribute something today that made someone else's life a little better?
- Am I making decisions that reflect my faith, even when it costs me something?

For another person, the values might be:

- **Creativity** – expressing ideas, building, innovating.
- **Community** – belonging to and building spaces where people feel seen.
- **Excellence** – doing work with care and integrity.

Their metrics will look different:

- Did I create today, or did I only consume?
- Did I deepen or invest in meaningful relationships, or did I isolate?
- Did I give my best to the work in front of me, or did I cut corners?

You might value adventure, learning, justice, beauty, stewardship, or mentoring the next generation. Whatever those core values are, they must become the metrics by which you measure success, not someone else's scoreboard. When your days, weeks, and years begin to reflect what you say you value, you are living in alignment. When they don't, it's a sign you may be drifting toward a borrowed dream.

Clarifying your alignment metrics is how you keep yourself honest. It is how you discern whether what you're doing truly aligns with who you are and your unique purpose, or whether you are performing for a position that does not match what you value.

This chapter was designed to pull you into deep introspection—to slow you down long enough to question whether what you're pursuing, and how you're pursuing it, actually aligns with what matters most to your unique assignment. Because ultimately, the goal is to live a life of power, from power, that produces power in others. Power, in this sense, is the byproduct of alignment—of who you are, what you are doing, and who you are doing it for, all intersecting with what you value.

From that place, you refuse to live a life borrowed from other people's expectations and instead live a life that is true to the assignment placed on your life. Because one of the scariest realizations we can ever have is to arrive at the end of our lives and discover that we may have lived someone else's.

And as we move forward, the natural next question becomes: How do I begin, from this place of clarity, to live with intention—using the gift of my attention to align my daily choices with the life I'm called to live?

CHAPTER TEN

LIVING WITH INTENTION

ONE OF THE most sobering questions you can ask yourself is not simply, "What am I doing with my life?" but, "How did I arrive at the life I'm currently living?" When you slow down long enough to reflect, you begin to realize that the life you are living right now—your routines, your relationships, your work, your sense of joy or frustration—is not random. It is the cumulative result of choices you have made, choices that were made for you, and plans you either brought into your days or allowed your days to hand to you.

In the last chapter, we talked about borrowed dreams and broken metrics—how easy it is to run full steam toward a destination that was never designed for you, using someone else's scoreboard to measure your life. The natural next step is this: once you begin to reclaim your dream and reset your metrics around alignment and purpose, how do you actually live your life differently, day by day? That question brings us to the power of intention.

I firmly believe that if you do not go into your day with a plan, your day will gladly give you one. Days are not neutral. They arrive already loaded with emails, notifications, demands, crises, and expectations. You wake up, glance at your phone "for a second," and before you know it you've answered three messages, reacted to two emails, scrolled through a feed that tells you what everyone else is doing with their lives, and you're already behind on what you said mattered to you. Multiply that by weeks and months, and you can wake up in a life that you never intentionally designed, but faithfully maintained.

This chapter is about disrupting that drift.

My desire is to help you understand how to live with intention—to design, on purpose, the life you desire to see, and to do so in a way that is deeply aligned with who you are and what you're here to impact. Not a life that just looks good on paper, but a life that feels congruent in your soul.

YOUR LIFE IS RESPONDING TO CHOICES

Before we talk about designing anything, we have to confront a foundational reality: what you do matters. What you do in this life matters. What you do on a daytoday basis matters. You are not at the mercy of fate, personality tests, or other people's decisions. You have been given the dignity and responsibility of choice.

The life you are living right now is the culmination of choices made for you and choices made by you. That can feel heavy if you stop there, especially if you can point to moments where you didn't have much say. But there needs to be a comma in that sentence.

Because the life you can live from this point forward can also be the byproduct of choices made by you. You can decide that today becomes a pivot point instead of just another repeat of yesterday. You can begin to introduce new inputs that align with the outcomes you say you want to see.

Living with intention begins when you accept that your days are not simply something you pass through; they are something you participate in creating. Intention is you stepping into that creative role with your eyes open.

So how do you actually do that? How do you live intentionally and design the life you desire? The talk I gave on this outlined four core principles, and I want to expand on them here:

1.   Commit to an unshakable value system.
2.   Let impact become your starting question.
3.   Start where you are and build a bridge with strategy.
4.   Understand that intention grows in immersion.

Let's walk through each of these together.

1. COMMIT TO AN UNSHAKABLE VALUE SYSTEM

The first principle is deceptively simple and deeply consequential: you must commit to an unshakable value system.

We love language like "design the life you desire," but we don't slow down enough to examine that word—desire. Desire can be beautiful, but it can also be dangerous. You can desire things that feel good to you in the short term but quietly destroy your legacy in the long term. You can yearn with your whole heart for something and still be yearning for the wrong thing.

Desire, by itself, is not a trustworthy compass.

You cannot build your life only on what you feel like in the moment. You need a value system—a deeper foundation that shapes and filters your desires before they ever become goals. Your values, not your moods, should be the soil from which your desires grow.

For me, that value system is grounded in my faith. The principles I live by—how I treat people, how I lead, how I make decisions—flow out of a conviction that there is a Creator who is both origin and standard. My faith is not just a motivational quote I turn to when it's convenient; it is the foundation I choose to build my life on.

For you, the question becomes: what value system are you building your life on?

Are your values simply handmedowns from your family or culture, never examined, just assumed? Or are your values rooted in truth and principle—things like treating others the way you want to be treated, telling the truth even when it costs you something, loving people, serving, owning your growth instead of deflecting responsibility?

Your value system is the engine behind your desires.

Here is the chain I want you to see clearly:

Values fuel desire, desire sets your focus, focus directs your attention, and attention builds your priorities. Change the values at the root, and the entire tree of your life begins to shift.

If your values are shaky, everything downstream becomes shaky as well.

If you value status more than integrity, you will desire recognition more than growth, focus on image more than substance, and give your attention to things that keep you visible but not necessarily valuable. Your priorities will reflect that.

If you value comfort more than calling, you will desire ease more than impact, focus on avoiding pain instead of pursuing purpose, and give your attention to what numbs you rather than what builds you. Your priorities will reflect that, too.

However, when your values are grounded—when you decide, for example, that you value character, contribution, and alignment with your assignment above mere convenience or popularity—your desires begin to shift. You stop chasing what simply looks good and start craving what is genuinely good for you and those connected to you. As your desires change, your focus, your attention, and your priorities begin to reorganize themselves around those values.

Living with intention, then, is not just about timeblocking or habit tracking. It begins with the quiet, courageous work of asking,

"What do I truly value, and is the life I am currently living actually built on those values or on someone else's?"

2. LET IMPACT BECOME YOUR STARTING QUESTION

Values answer the question, "What kind of person am I becoming?" The next principle answers, "What am I becoming for?"

Most people, when they decide they want to transform their life, start with achievement questions:

- What do I want to accomplish?
- What do I want to have?
- What do I want my life to look like in five years?

Those are not wrong questions, but if they are your starting point, you are very likely to drift back into borrowed dreams, measuring your life by someone else's metrics. I believe the question that should come first is this:

What impact do I want to make with my life?

Impact reframes everything.

Earlier in this book, I talked about losing my father—one of the deepest losses I have ever walked through. At his celebration of life, nobody stood up to talk about the brands of clothing he preferred, the cars he drove, or the square footage of his house. Person after person, in their own words, talked about one thing: his impact. The way he showed up, the encouragement he gave, the sacrifices he made, the way his life rippled into theirs.

To this day, when his name is mentioned back home in the Caribbean, you don't just think of a man who had things; you think of a man who made a difference. That moment reframed success for me. The real secret to a successful life is a life lived to make an impact. Impact is intimate. It is about significance, not just size.

We tend to think impact means doing something on a massive scale, but the truth is, impact is about alignment with your assignment. Your assignment in this season might be to be a present parent, a faithful steward of your healing, a strategic leader of a small team, or the person in your friend group who finally says, "Let's stop talking about people and start talking about purpose." None of that is small if it is aligned.

Living with intention means impact becomes your compass. Before you say yes to an opportunity, set a goal, or fill your calendar, you begin with questions like:

- What kind of impact do I want my life to make in this season?
- Who am I called to impact right now—my family, my team, my clients, my community, my own soul?
- If impact, not ego, guided my decisions this year, what would stay and what would have to go?

When impact is your starting question, success becomes more than accumulation. It becomes alignment with the difference you were born to make.

3. START WHERE YOU ARE: STRATEGY AS THE BRIDGE

Once you begin to clarify your values and your desired impact, the temptation is to reach for drastic change overnight. We want to burn everything down and start over. But the third principle is both humbling and liberating: you must start where you are.

Many of us quietly believe, "I can start living intentionally when I have more money, more time, more support, more clarity, more confidence." We treat the life we want as something that can only begin once conditions outside of us shift. Until then, we say we are "waiting"—but often, we are avoiding.

Design—the kind of design we are talking about here—is not fantasy. Design is taking the pieces you currently have and, over time, constructing a masterpiece. It is learning how to use what is already in your hands to move toward what you see in your heart.

You cannot build the next level of your life while secretly despising your current level. If you refuse to embrace where you are, you will try to move forward while constantly staring at what you lack. That inner conflict will eventually exhaust you.

Embracing where you are does not mean settling there. It means acknowledging reality so that strategy has something solid to work with. A strategy that ignores reality is just a fantasy written in bullet points.

I like to think of it this way:

- Dreams are the pictures of what you desire.
- Reality is where you currently stand.
- Strategy is the bridge that connects the two.

Living with intention means you become a builder of bridges, not just a collector of dreams.

Here's a simple way to begin that process in any area of your life:

1. Choose one area you care about right now—your finances, your health, your relationships, your spiritual life, your work.
2. Write one honest sentence about your current reality in that area. No spin, no shame, just truth.
3. Write one realistic next action you can take in the next seven days that would move you one step closer to the life you desire in that area. Not ten steps, not the perfect plan—just one clear, doable action.

It might look like:

"I am carrying more debt than feels peaceful." □ "This week I will list every debt I have and schedule a 30minute block to create a simple payoff plan."

or

"My marriage feels distant." □ "This week I will initiate one honest conversation with my spouse and schedule a time for us to be together without distractions."

The reason most dreams go unrealized is not because people don't dream; it's because they never build a bridge between dream and reality through strategy. They hope, they wish, they vision board—but they do not design.

Intention is not about shaming yourself for where you are. It's about finally telling yourself the truth so you can move forward from a place of clarity instead of illusion.

4. INTENTION GROWS IN IMMERSION

The fourth principle may be the one we underestimate most: intention grows in immersion.

You can have a clear value system, a desire to make impact, and a realistic strategy—and still feel stuck. Often that's because your daily environment is quietly working against your intention. You are trying to live a new life while staying fully immersed in old patterns, old conversations, and old atmospheres.

Immersion is about what you sit in, dwell in, and surround yourself with. If you want to live with intention, you must immerse yourself in things that feed that intention:

- Reading and studying content that stretches your thinking and strengthens your spirit.
- Being in circles and relationships that challenge you to rise instead of constantly pulling you back into old narratives.
- Joining communities, groups, and environments that look like where you're going, not just where you've been.

I have watched this play out in my own life and in the lives of clients. Someone decides they want to grow in leadership, so they start immersing themselves in books on leadership, join a mastermind, and intentionally spend time around leaders who live what they teach. Over time, without forcing it, their language begins to shift. The way they think about problems changes. Their standards rise. That is immersion at work.

On the flip side, if you say you want a life of healthy relationships but remain immersed in gossip, cynicism, and surfacelevel interactions, your intention will suffocate. If you say you want to build a business but never immerse yourself in learning, mentorship, or communities of builders, your intention will stay trapped in your notes app.

The conflict between your stated desires and your daily immersion will always create tension. Over time, that tension will either pull you back into autopilot or propel you forward into change.

Intention cannot grow in isolation from your environment. It grows when, repeatedly and intentionally, you place yourself in spaces that reflect who you are becoming.

ATTENTION: THE EVERYDAY EXPRESSION OF INTENTION

If intention is the internal decision to live your life on purpose, attention is how that decision shows up in real time. Attention is where your eyes go, where your mind rests, where your energy flows when nobody is assigning tasks to you.

This is where the last chapter and this one intersect so tightly: borrowed dreams are revealed by how you spend your attention. You can say you value impact, but your attention might still be consumed by comparison. You can say you value family, but your attention might still be monopolized by work that gives you quicker validation than the slow, sacred work of presence.

Living with intention through the gift of attention means you begin to ask yourself, multiple times a day:

- Is what I'm giving my attention to right now aligned with the life I say I am designing?
- Does this scroll, this conversation, this task, this thought pattern move me toward my values and impact—or away from them?

This isn't about micromanaging every minute. It's about training your attention to serve your intention instead of sabotaging it.

You will still have responsibilities, deadlines, and obligations. The goal is not to escape those, but to move through them differently—to be more present where you are, to prioritize what matters within them, and to guard the spaces that feed your soul and your assignment. Living with intention is not a onetime declaration; it is a daily practice of alignment.

- You clarify your values, so your desires have a trustworthy foundation.
- You start with impact, so success is measured by alignment with your assignment, not just accumulation.
- You start where you are, embracing reality so that strategy can build a bridge between here and where you're called to go.

- You immerse yourself in environments and relationships that support who you're becoming, because intention grows in immersion.
- And you steward your attention, moment by moment, as the everyday proof of what you truly intend to become.

When these pieces begin to work together, you move out of autopilot and into alignment. Your life stops being something that simply happens to you and starts becoming something that is happening through you—for the sake of the impact you were created to make.

And as you live with that level of intention, another tension inevitably rises: the tension between your desire to give your all and your need to remain whole. How do you pursue purpose passionately without sacrificing your health, your relationships, or your soul on the altar of productivity? To answer that, we need to talk about why balance is seasonal, not static, and how to honor your limits without abandoning your assignment.

CHAPTER ELEVEN

BEATING BURNOUT WITH BALANCE

IN THE LAST chapter, we talked about living with intention—about designing your life from a place of clarity instead of drifting into a life that just "happened" to you. But there is a hard truth we have to confront on the other side of intention: you can be incredibly intentional, deeply committed to impact, and still be quietly burning yourself to the ground. You can be clear on your values and assignments and yet be living in a way that slowly erodes your capacity to carry those very assignments well.

Living on purpose means nothing if the way you are living is killing you.

That's why we need to talk about burnout and balance—not as trendy words, but as real forces that shape whether you can sustain the life you are intentionally designing.

WHEN EXCELLENCE MEETS EMPTY

I wish I could say I only studied burnout from the outside, as a coach and speaker helping other people navigate it. I can't. I found myself in one of the most critical seasons of burnout I've ever walked through—one that almost cost me my health.

I was in a stretch where I was everywhere. Planes, hotels, green rooms, stages. From keynote to keynote, from coaching session to coaching session, from strategy calls to content creation to writing articles and mapping out new programs, the list could go on. The brand was growing quickly, opportunities were opening, and expectations—my own and others'—were multiplying. Somewhere in the middle of that momentum, I slowly began to dehumanize my own needs. I treated my body like a machine that only existed to carry my calling.

I wasn't just tired; I was severely burnt out. I was taking care of everything and everyone else and neglecting myself. My average blood pressure hovered around 180/90. That was not a onetime spike; it was a constant. I normalized it. I convinced myself it was manageable, that it was simply the "cost" of the life I was building. Over a few months, I gained about sixty pounds. I was still standing on stages, still effective in my ability to communicate and connect, but I was no longer doing it from a healthy place.

Eventually the burnout caught up with me. I knew I was giving "good enough," but it was no longer my absolute best. I wasn't serving from abundance and overflow; I was serving from depletion and empty. Some of the people closest to me started to notice a subtle falloff in my effectiveness—not in the gift itself, but in the energy behind it. I've always believed you can reach a point where your gift still functions in a way that looks impressive to others, but it's no longer the most effective expression of who you are when you are whole.

That's where I was.

At that point, a question started to haunt me: Am I operating from integrity if I'm operating from a version of myself that is not giving my absolute best, but settling for what others assume is good enough?

As I was working on this book, that question stopped being theoretical. I had just finished a video—a piece of content I felt good about—and I sent it to one of my brothers. Not a brother by blood, but by relationship. His response rocked me. He said, "Jovan, I've got to be honest with you. I personally can't find myself taking advice from a person who doesn't take their own health seriously."

Ouch doesn't even begin to describe it.

I'm going to share something here that I didn't share with him. Once he reads this, he'll know exactly who he is. My first response was to get defensive. I started typing a message fueled by anger and ego: "You have no idea what I've been going through. You don't know the pressure I've been under, the stress in my home, the weight of what I'm carrying. You haven't called to check on me, but you're quick to comment on my appearance." It would have been easy to justify that response based on our relational dynamic.

But as quickly as I typed the message, I deleted it. I sat in the airport parking lot, in the cold, replaying his words. It hurt. But I had to ask myself a harder question than "How dare he?" I had to ask, Was he wrong?

The answer was no.

I pride myself on taking seriously the way I live behind the scenes. I never want my private life to contradict the message I deliver publicly. I am probably harder on myself than anyone else when it comes to living what I teach. But in that moment, I had to admit that—regardless of the reasons, regardless of the noble excuses of being "busy" pursuing, teaching, growing, and impacting—I had neglected myself.

My brother wasn't trying to hurt me. That comment ended up being one of the most significant gifts in that season, because he refused to simply validate my content. He loved me enough to challenge my condition. He finished his message with a sentence I'll never forget: "In order for you to do what you're doing at the highest level possible, what you look like is going to matter."

I didn't hear that as shallow. I heard it as accountability. It was a reminder that my life has to embody what I teach. Scripture says,

"Not many of you should become teachers, because those who teach will be held to a higher standard." I had to swallow my pride, call my brother the next morning, and say, "Thank you. Thank you for telling me what hurt." He admitted he'd wanted to say it for a while but didn't want me to take it personally. The truth is, I did—and I needed to.

As I write this, I'm fifteen pounds down and still moving in the right direction. For me, it was never just about the weight. The weight was an indicator, a visible manifestation of an internal reality: I had allowed myself to be depleted to the point where I was showing up for others out of repetition, but neglecting to show up for myself so that I could serve from my true essence.

I share this with you because, just like me, it is so easy to lose focus on being good while you are busy doing good. Burnout will disguise itself as productivity until you slow down long enough to notice that the cost is your vitality.

EXCELLENCE AND THE TRAP OF OVERDRIVE

Let's talk about why this can be so tricky for driven people.

When you study individuals who have made a significant impact—athletes, innovators, leaders, everyday people who live their assignment at a high level—one separating factor shows up over and over again: excellence. Excellence is what distinguishes good from great, ordinary from extraordinary, mediocre from exceptional.

I don't want you to go through life and only ever taste "good enough." I want you to step into a life that reflects the fullness of what's possible when you bring your whole self to the table. The worst life to live is a halflived one. And excellence is one of the ways we ensure we are not just existing, but fully engaging what this one life has to offer.

But here's the tension: if we misunderstand excellence, we will use it to justify burnout instead of elevating our impact.

In my talk on this, I outlined three principles around excellence that I believe are essential if we are going to embody it in a healthy way:

1. Excellence requires intentionality.
2. Excellence will stretch you.
3. You cannot execute with excellence on empty.

The first two principles are where high achievers usually nod along. The third is where many of us quietly fail.

Excellence doesn't happen by accident. It doesn't show up just because you roll out of bed and "do the do." You can go through the motions of something and never bring your full emotion, focus, or presence to it. Excellence happens when you show up with intention, not just at the appointment. It requires planning, strategy, thoughtful preparation, and the willingness to steward your attention, not just your time.

Excellence also stretches you. It pulls you past comfort zones, challenges your belief systems, and requires you to collaborate, learn, and evolve. It demands that you grow beyond what you have always done and how you have always thought, so you can execute and embody your role at a new level.

But none of that matters if you ignore the third principle: you can't execute with excellence on empty. You can sprint like a drag car—a burst of speed for a quarter mile—but if you want to run like a NASCAR, consistently at a high level over time, you must protect your vitality. You cannot keep burning the same tank and expect a different outcome.

This is where burnout enters the conversation.

UNDERSTANDING BURNOUT: THE COLLISION POINT

We throw the word "burnout" around so often that it can start to lose its weight. To address it, we have to define it.

Burnout is not just feeling tired. Burnout is the collision between physical fatigue and emotional fatigue. It is the place where your body is drained because you have been doing, going, and pushing, and your inner world is drained because you have been carrying weight—stress, expectations, relational complexity, unprocessed emotions—that your soul hasn't had space to process.

We must respect the fact that we are human. Your body needs rest. Sleep is not a luxury; it is maintenance. Your emotions need room. You cannot endlessly absorb other people's crises, demands, and projections without tending to your own heart. When physical fatigue and emotional fatigue collide, burnout happens.

You might still be walking. You might still be functioning. You might still be performing. But hear me: you may be able to walk in burnout, yet you cannot win in burnout. You cannot execute at the level you were designed to execute with excellence if you are constantly drawing from an empty internal account.

To overcome anything, you must first understand it. We cannot beat burnout by ignoring it, numbing it, or glorifying it as a sign of how committed we are. We beat burnout by bringing wisdom to it. Wisdom gives us the clarity and insight to approach life differently, not just more intensely.

So how do we beat burnout? We beat burnout with balance.

BALANCE: SEASONAL, NOT STATIC

Before we talk about how to achieve balance, we need to redefine it.

Many of us hear the word "balance" and picture a perfect, static image where every area of life gets equal time, equal energy, equal focus, every day. That picture is not only unrealistic; it's one of the reasons we feel like we're failing. Life does not move in straight lines; it moves in seasons.

In my definition, balance is the awareness of knowing what season you're in so that you can adjust in order to keep the main thing the main thing.

Balance is not rigidity—doing the same thing in the same way regardless of what is happening around you. That's not balance; that's stubbornness. True balance is fluid. It allows you to pivot with purpose. You're not changing for the sake of change; you are changing how you show up so that you can continue to honor your priorities in a shifting context.

Scripture says in Ecclesiastes that to everything there is a season and a time for every purpose under heaven—a time to be born and a time to die, to plant and to uproot, to weep and to laugh, to mourn and to dance, to embrace and to refrain from embracing, to keep and to cast away, to be silent and to speak. Life is seasons. Your business, your relationships, your inner life, your calling—they all move through different seasons.

Balance is learning to read the season you are in and then adjusting your expectations and energy so you can keep the main thing the main thing in that season.

The problem is, many of us are in a new season but still showing up with the strategy of the old one. Our expectations have changed, but our approach hasn't. So we keep trying to carry yesterday's schedule into today's demands and wonder why we feel burnt out.

To beat burnout with balance, I believe there are three essential skills you must cultivate:

1. Awareness
2. Adaptability
3. Discipline

AWARENESS: NAMING THE SEASON YOU'RE IN

The first step in protecting balance is awareness—the willingness to pause long enough to ask, "What season am I actually in?"

Awareness means you stop living only by default and start paying attention to what is actually happening in and around you. Maybe this is a season where your professional life requires more bandwidth—big projects, launches, new responsibilities. Maybe it's a season where your personal life is frontloaded—aging parents, young children, a health journey, grief, or healing work that demands extra energy.

If you don't pause to acknowledge the season, you will hold yourself to expectations that don't match your current reality. You will judge yourself by a standard that might have made sense two years ago, but is completely misaligned with the weight of this moment.

Awareness doesn't appear magically. It is cultivated. In my own life and in the lives of the people I coach, awareness grows through practices like:

- Taking intentional pauses instead of moving from task to task without breathing.
- Journaling honestly about what's working, what's not, and what you're feeling.
- Engaging in prayer or meditation to recenter your heart and hear what you might be avoiding.
- Checking your "internal dashboard"—asking yourself, How is my body? How is my mind? How is my heart?

Without awareness, you will keep saying yes at a pace your soul can't sustain. With awareness, you begin to see clearly enough to make different choices.

ADAPTABILITY: PIVOTING WITH PURPOSE

The second skill is adaptability. Once you know what season you're in, the question becomes: "What adjustments do I need to make to remain faithful to my priorities in this season?"

Adaptability does not mean compromising your authenticity. It doesn't mean becoming a different person. It means being willing to pivot the way you show up so you can still honor why you're showing up. It is pivoting with purpose.

In some seasons, adaptation might look like:

- Saying yes to more professional bandwidth while temporarily simplifying your social calendar.
- Reducing the number of projects you're leading so you can be more present at home.
- Adjusting your workout schedule instead of abandoning your health entirely because life got busy.

If your professional world is demanding more of you right now, that automatically means you have less bandwidth personally. Balance is not pretending that's not true; it's adjusting your personal expectations so you can sustain your professional commitments without crumbling.

The question is not, "How do I keep doing everything at the same level?" The question is, "What is the main thing in this season, and what needs to shift so I can keep the main thing the main thing?"

Adaptability requires humility. It asks you to release perfection and embrace what is actually possible, not what looks impressive on paper. It is choosing strategic pivots so that you can finish, not just start, what matters.

DISCIPLINE: PROTECTING BOUNDARIES AND VITALITY

The third skill may be the hardest: discipline.

Once you have awareness and adaptability, discipline is what protects the changes you know you need to make. Discipline is not only about waking up early or hustling harder. In this context, discipline is the willingness to honor your boundaries even when it disappoints people.

To live with healthy balance, you must develop the discipline to be at peace with the fact that some people will want you to show up in ways that work for them but compromise you. Discipline says, "I can love you and still say no."

I heard it said—and I believe it was Brené Brown—that boundaries are the way I'm able to love you and me simultaneously. Boundaries are not walls to keep people out; they are lines that protect what matters most so that your yes remains meaningful.

Discipline looks like:

- Stopping work at a certain time even when there is more to do, because your rest and relationships are not optional.
- Saying no to "good" opportunities that would pull you away from your primary assignment in this season.
- Choosing to rest at the halfway point of your tank instead of waiting until you are completely empty.

This last point is critical. Most of us treat empty as our threshold for rest. We only slow down when we are forced to. We run on fumes, then collapse, then call that "normal." But it is dangerous to live like that. When you continually operate on empty, you don't just become exhausted; you become bitter. You start resenting the very people you're serving, because you are giving what you do not have to give.

I want to challenge you to change your threshold for burnout. Imagine your energy and vitality like a glass of water. Every expectation, conversation, decision, responsibility, and assignment takes something out of that glass. Instead of waiting until the glass is empty to rest, what if you decided that your threshold is halfway?

What if, when you noticed yourself reaching the midpoint, you chose to pause, replenish, and reset? Not because you're weak, but because you are valuable. Because you cannot execute with sustainable excellence if you only ever stop when you're on the verge of collapse.

FROM DEPLETION TO OVERFLOW

Beating burnout with balance is not about becoming less committed or lowering your standards. It's about honoring the reality that you cannot carry a big assignment with a neglected soul.

When I look back at that season of burnout in my own life—the high blood pressure, the weight gain, the constant travel, the performance on stage paired with the depletion off stage—I realize I wasn't betraying my calling because I didn't care. I was betraying my calling because I refused to admit I was human.

My brother's words forced me to realign. They reminded me that excellence is not just what people see when I hold a microphone; it's also how I treat the vessel holding the message. Balance became more than a concept. It became a necessary commitment if I wanted to still be standing, still whole, still impactful years from now.

As you think about your own life, I want you to consider a few questions:

- Where have you normalized exhaustion and called it "the grind"?
- What is your body trying to tell you that your schedule keeps ignoring?
- What season are you actually in, and where do your expectations need to shift to match it?

- What boundaries have you been afraid to set because you don't want to disappoint people?

Living with intention, as we explored in the last chapter, is about designing your life around your values and desired impact. Living with balance is about sustaining that design without losing yourself in the process.

When awareness, adaptability, and discipline begin to work together, burnout loses its grip. You stop wearing depletion as a badge of honor. You start honoring rest as a strategic decision, not a sign of laziness. You begin contributing from overflow instead of scraping the bottom of an empty barrel.

And perhaps most importantly, you begin to live in a way where the people who experience your gift also get to experience your presence—fully alive, not just barely making it.

In the chapters ahead, we will keep building on this foundation, exploring how excellence and impact can flow from a life that is aligned, intentional, and whole—not perfect, but integrated. For now, I want you to remember this: you cannot execute with excellence on empty, and you are too valuable to keep living at war with your own vitality.

CHAPTER TWELVE

THE HABITS THAT SHAPE A FULFILLED LIFE

LOVE IS NOT just something you feel; it is something you choose to build toward. When I talk about success, I'm not talking about a title, a bank balance, or a social media highlight reel. My definition of success is this: success is the achievement of a harmonious love life—a life you actually love living, not just a life other people applaud.

When most people hear "love life," they immediately think of romance. They think about the love they share with someone else. That kind of love matters, but it is only part of the picture. The love life I'm talking about is broader and deeper. It is the life you are constructing—day by day—that you genuinely love. The life where who you are, what you do, and how you do it are not at war with each other.

To understand that kind of life, I want to give you two words: realization and synchronization. Realization is about the fulfillment of your purpose and potential. Synchronization is about alignment between your internal satisfaction and your external goals.

When realization is present, you are not just existing. You're using your gifts, talents, and abilities in ways that matter. When synchronization is present, you are not sacrificing your inner peace for outer success, or vice versa. You are refusing to choose between achievement and alignment.

My conviction is simple: you are meant to build a life where purpose and potential are realized, and where internal satisfaction and external goals are synchronized, not constantly fighting each other. And that doesn't happen by accident. It happens through clarity, intention, and daily habits.

PURPOSE, POTENTIAL, AND WHAT YOU VALUE

Let's talk about purpose for a moment, because "build a life you love" can sound vague until we define it. Purpose is not just doing something you're good at. It's not just doing what pays well, or what impresses other people. Purpose, in this context, is using your gifts and abilities in opportunities that align with what you value.

Read that again.

You can operate in a space where you're not in your purpose and not operating at your potential. You can also operate in a space where you are in your purpose but not operating at your potential—underplaying, underpreparing, undercommitting. Or you can operate at your potential—using everything you have—but in an area that has nothing to do with your true purpose.

The sweet spot, the place where a life you love becomes possible, is where:

- You are in your purpose: using your gifts in the right arena.
- You are operating at your potential: not shrinking, not coasting.

- You are aligned with your values: not betraying what matters to you in order to look successful.

Most people don't discover this sweet spot in a moment. They bump into it, back away from it, and slowly grow into it. I've watched leaders live in each of these quadrants. I've seen the executive who was wildly talented, but in an industry that never aligned with their convictions. They were operating at high potential, but outside their purpose. Their calendar was full, their resume impressive, but every promotion felt like being rewarded for playing the wrong game.

I've also met people who were clearly in their purpose but hiding inside it. They loved the work, they loved the people, but they were playing small—volunteering when they should have been leading, preparing the room when they were called to be on the stage. They were in the right arena, but they were running half-speed because disappointment, fear, or comparison convinced them that allout effort was too risky.

Then there are those seasons where you're out of purpose and out of potential. You're doing just enough to get by, going through the motions in spaces that don't require your best and don't reflect your values. Those are the seasons where your life starts to feel numb—not because nothing is happening, but because nothing that matters to you is happening through you.

Building the life you love is the journey of moving toward that sweet spot and staying there long enough to see the fruit. It is a slow, faithful recalibration where your gifts, your effort, and your values finally start telling the same story about who you are becoming.

But vision alone won't get you there. Passion alone won't get you there. Even clarity alone won't get you there. This is where habits come in—not as rigid rules, but as daily practices that turn your vision into reality.

WHY HABITS MATTER FOR A LIFE YOU LOVE

If you win the morning, you win the day. If you win enough days, you win the week, then the month, then the year—and eventually, you win in life. All of that winning begins with the tone you set for your day.

A fulfilled, lovefilled life is not the result of one big decision. It is the compound interest of what you repeatedly choose when no one is watching. Your daily habits are quiet agreements you've made with your future. They determine whether you live from overflow or from empty, from alignment or from constant reaction.

In earlier chapters, we talked about burnout, misalignment, and the danger of living in patterns that feel normal but aren't healthy. Here, I want to show you how three simple habits can quietly retrain those patterns from the inside out. Building a life you love is where we begin to flip that script. Here, we take everything you've learned about undercurrents, beliefs, and reflection and anchor it in three daily habits:

- Purposeful preparation
- Quiet contemplation
- Consistent commitment

These habits are not about perfection. They are about direction. They help you live in a way that is congruent with your purpose, your potential, and your values.

HABIT 1: PURPOSEFUL PREPARATION

Purposeful preparation is the practice of entering your day with a plan instead of a hope. It is you deciding, before the noise starts, what will matter most. It says, "I refuse to surrender my day to randomness or other people's urgency."

Without preparation, your day belongs to whoever or whatever shouts the loudest: emails, notifications, other people's crises, your own distractions. You may end the day exhausted and still feel like you didn't move anything that truly matters. That's the fastest way to build a life you don't love—one that looks productive but feels hollow.

Purposeful preparation doesn't require an elaborate ritual. I like to frame it in sevenminute increments. Seven focused minutes each morning to step away from autopilot and ask:

- What truly matters today?
- What must get my best energy?
- What can wait, and what needs to be released?

Those seven minutes move through three simple steps:

Review

Look briefly at yesterday. Where did you feel aligned? Where did you feel off? What drained you? What energized you?

Refine

Define your top three mustwins for today—three outcomes that, if achieved, would make today meaningful. Then decide what can be delegated, delayed, or deleted.

Reinforce

Ask: "How does today serve the life I'm building?" Connect your tasks to your larger vision of a life you love, to your purpose and values.

Let me give you a picture. Imagine waking up on a Wednesday that you already know will be full—backtoback meetings, family responsibilities, a looming deadline. Without preparation, the day owns you before your feet hit the floor. But with seven minutes of purposeful preparation, the shape of the day changes.

You review yesterday and realize every time you checked your phone between meetings, your anxiety spiked and your focus dipped. You refine your mustwins: one key client conversation, one focused block on your project, and one intentional moment with your family before the day ends. You reinforce it by reminding yourself that these three moments are not just tasks—they are expressions of the life you are building, the kind of leader and partner you are becoming.

The schedule might still be full, but now your effort has a target. You are not just surviving the day; you are shaping it.

You will almost always hit, or come close to, what you aim at. If you aim at nothing, you will also hit it—or come close. Purposeful preparation is how you choose your aim in advance.

It also protects you from a subtle trap: disguised distraction.

You cannot be distracted by what you're not attracted to. Most of your distractions don't show up as obviously trivial. They show up as opportunities, as people you care about, as good things that are simply not the right things for this season.

When you've already decided your priorities, you can say no with integrity. You're not rejecting people; you're respecting your purpose and the life you're building.

HABIT 2: QUIET CONTEMPLATION

If purposeful preparation sets your direction, quiet contemplation protects your disposition. It is the habit of intentionally quieting external noise so you can hear your internal voice—the voice of conviction, wisdom, and, for many of us, the voice of God.

Quiet contemplation is not a luxury. It is a necessity if you want to build a life you love. Without it, you live as a reactor, constantly pulled by circumstance and emotion. With it, you learn to move through chaos without letting chaos move through you.

In quiet contemplation, you:

- Step away from everyone else's expectations.
- Anchor your peace before the day starts tugging on it.
- Listen for what your spirit is saying beneath your schedule and your striving.

This silence can feel uncomfortable at first because it exposes what you really believe. Thoughts surface—fears, insecurities, unresolved questions. Most of us have learned to outrun those thoughts with constant noise. But if you never listen, you never lead yourself. You simply drift.

Quiet contemplation gives you a chance to notice the stories you're living out of:

"I'm behind."
"I have to prove myself today."
"If I slow down, everything will fall apart."

Once you see them, you can respond differently. You can ask, "Is this actually true, or just familiar?" That alone can change the trajectory of your day.

You can practice quiet contemplation in different ways:

- Stillness and breathing: Sit, breathe slowly, and focus on a grounding phrase. When your mind wanders—and it will—gently bring it back. Ten minutes can soften the edges of an entire day.
- Journaling as conversation: Write down what weighs on you, what you need to release, what you're grateful for, and who you want to be as you move through the day.
- Walking contemplation: Take a slow walk without headphones. Notice your surroundings. Ask yourself, "Where am I really, and what needs to shift?"

Quiet contemplation allows you to step into the day from a place of peace instead of going into the day looking for peace in people, possessions, or performance. You become the originator of peace, not a constant consumer of it.

When you love the life you are building, protecting your peace becomes nonnegotiable. You realize that nothing is worth losing yourself.

HABIT 3: CONSISTENT COMMITMENT

Motivation is a spark; commitment is the engine. Motivation feels incredible, but it is also inconsistent. If you build your life on how you feel, your progress will always be fragile. Consistent commitment says, "Even when the excitement fades, my actions won't."

This habit is about small, meaningful actions you repeat daily—especially when you're tired, bored, or tempted to quit. It asks:

- What promises am I making to myself?
- Which of those promises do I actually keep?
- What am I willing to do even on my worst day?

Most people don't abandon their dreams in one dramatic moment. They abandon them in quiet, incremental ways:

- Hitting snooze six times "just this once."
- Telling themselves, "I'll start next week," over and over.
- Breaking small promises to themselves and calling it "no big deal."

These microquits seem harmless, but they slowly erode selftrust. When you don't trust yourself, you dream smaller, ask for less, and settle faster.

Consistent commitment is built on microkeeps: small promises you keep to yourself every day. Over time, they change how you see yourself. You move from, "I'm trying to be disciplined" to, "I am someone who follows through."

To practice consistent commitment, design three categories of daily nonnegotiables:

Health NonNegotiable:

One simple, doable action you take for your body—walking, stretching, hydration, or movement.

Mind/Heart NonNegotiable

One action that strengthens your inner world—reading, prayer, meditation, journaling, learning for 10–15 minutes.

Mission/Impact NonNegotiable

One action that moves your calling forward—reaching out to someone, creating something, solving one meaningful problem.

Choose actions small enough to do on your bad days, not just your good days. That's how compound impact is built.

Imagine a week where you've picked your three nonnegotiables. Monday is smooth; you hit all three early. Wednesday falls apart; you're exhausted and tempted to skip everything. Instead, you walk around the block, read a few pages, and send one sincere message. Friday is messy again, but the pattern holds—you keep your promises, even at the smallest level.

By the end of the week, something powerful has shifted. Your circumstances may not have transformed yet, but your identity has started to. You are becoming the kind of person who shows up, especially for you.

INVENTORY: THE HABITS YOU ALREADY LIVE BY

Before you install new habits, you have to tell yourself the truth about the habits you already have. You are already a person of habit. The real question is: Are my habits helping me build a life I love, or are they quietly building a life I resent?

For one week, I want you to do a simple audit:

- Morning: What do you do in the first 60–90 minutes after waking? Where does your attention go?
- Afternoon: How do you handle your energy and focus? When are you most prone to distraction?
- Evening: How do you wind down? Are you numbing or nourishing?

Write it down without judgment; this is reflection without shame applied to your daily rhythms. At the end of the week, ask:

- Which habit, if changed, would create the biggest positive ripple?
- Which habit is clearly feeding burnout, anxiety, or emptiness?
- Which habit is already lifegiving and needs to be protected?

Awareness always comes before adjustment. You cannot build a life you love while lying to yourself about the life you are living.

Realization + Synchronization + Habits

Building a life you love is not about perfection. It is about integration—bringing together:

- Your purpose (where your gifts meet opportunities that align with your values).
- Your potential (the fullness of what you are capable of when you don't shrink).
- Your internal satisfaction (peace, joy, alignment).
- Your external goals (impact, provision, influence).

And then anchoring all of that in daily habits that support, rather than sabotage, that integration.

Purposeful preparation aligns your day with your vision. Quiet contemplation protects your inner world while you move toward it. Consistent commitment carries you when motivation can't.

That is how realization and synchronization move from theory into testimony. And this matters deeply when life does not go the way you planned. When adversity hits and disappointment shows up, these habits become your anchor. They will not erase the pain, but they will keep you from abandoning your purpose, shrinking your potential, or betraying your values in reaction to a hard moment.

If your mind can conceive this, and your heart will believe it, your hands can create the life, impact, love, and legacy you desire. Start where you are. Choose how you will prepare, how you will protect your peace, and which small commitments you will honor—no matter what.

Then do it again tomorrow.

CHAPTER THIRTEEN
ADVERSITY AS AN ALLY

*Adversity will shake you; the decision
you make in that moment determines
whether it breaks you or builds you.*

I DON'T THINK I've ever met a truly great person who didn't also carry a story of great pain. It's as though the drive and ambition to achieve extraordinary things often begin at the intersection of adversity and longing—a place where something painful happened, and a decision had to be made about what that pain would mean.

But it's not just that people with great pain accomplish big things. It's how they do it. They move with authenticity. They walk with empathy. They lead with a tenderness you don't get from an easy life. The adversity doesn't just push them to achieve; it shapes their hearts in the process.

In this chapter, I want to talk about adversity.

This isn't theoretical for me. The adversity in my life became the launching pad for the purpose I now live. I believe I was created, formed, and set apart for this work—but it was adversity that woke me up to the urgency of that assignment.

Nothing puts life in perspective quite like pain.

WHEN YOUR PROTECTOR THROWS YOU INTO THE DEEP

One of the defining moments of my life is a story I don't usually lead with, because of how it lands the first time people hear it. But if we're going to walk through transformation together, we might as well dive in headfirst. You'll see why that word matters in a minute.

At the age of nine, if you had asked me what my father had done to me, I might have told you he was guilty of attempted manslaughter—for trying to drown me. That's how dramatic it felt in my young mind. My father—my protector, my provider, the one responsible for nurturing me—threw me into the ocean.

Take a second and sit with that.

When I tell this story, people usually respond in one of a few ways:

- "Wait, what did you just say?"
- "Oh my goodness, that's horrible. Why would he do that?"
- A blank stare, unsure what emotion fits something that sounds so traumatic.
- Or my favorite: an awkward laugh, praying I'm joking.

Before you join nineyearold me in sentencing my father for a crime he didn't commit, let me give you the full picture.

Again, I grew up on the island of Antigua—home to 365 beaches, at least that's what we were told. Whether or not anyone has actually counted, we're known for our water. The idea of growing up there and not being able to swim is almost a kind of cultural betrayal. It's like being a passionate vegan caught sneaking ChickfilA, or living in America and knowing nothing about football. It just doesn't fit.

At nine years old, that was me. Your boy could not swim. And everybody knew it. So my father decided it was his responsibility to make sure his son wasn't the black sheep of the island.

He took me to the beach with my floaties—my comfort, my certainty, my safety net. Then he did something I did not appreciate at the time: he took them off. Those floaties had been with me for years. Taking them away felt like stripping me of the little confidence I had.

He stretched his arms out in front of him like a bed and said, "Son, I need you to listen carefully. Lay on my hands." I climbed onto his arms reluctantly. Then he said, "Move your feet like a scuba diver. Now move your arms back and forth like you're reaching for something in front of you—right hand, then left, and repeat."

I did exactly what he said.

With every stroke, my belief grew. With every kick, my confidence increased. I felt free. I felt like I had discovered a new version of myself.

Then he said, "Okay, stop. Great job! You think you got it?"

With the biggest smile, I said, "Yes, Daddy, I do." Those were my last peaceful words before he tossed me—about six feet—toward the deeper water.

Time slowed down. I saw the grin on his face. I felt betrayed. My brain was screaming, What is happening? Then I hit the water and panic took over. Think Titanic, when the ship finally goes under and everyone is fighting for their lives—that's how it felt in my nine-yearold mind.

In the middle of my fear, I heard his voice:

"Hey! Relax. Do what I just taught you. Move your feet like a scuba diver and your arms back and forth. All you need to do is get to me, and you'll be okay."

I had a decision to make: sink or swim.

I chose to swim. It wasn't pretty or polished, but that didn't matter. What mattered was that I was determined to get to my father by any means necessary. After a few strokes, I felt his hands grab me and pull me in. "Great job, son! You did it. You made it. You swam!"

At first, I didn't share his excitement. I was still dealing with the emotional residue of the moment. But as my mind caught up, my fear turned into understanding. This wasn't an attempt to drown me. It was a calculated decision to throw me into a situation that forced me to discover my capacity.

My father knew something about adversity:

when we are put in uncomfortable, even scary situations, we have the gift of response. If we choose to respond, we unlock potential we didn't know we had.

I didn't realize it then, but that moment would become one of the metaphors for my life:

Sometimes the only way to discover you can swim is to be thrown into the deep.

WHEN ADVERSITY BECOMES PERSONAL: LOSING MY FATHER

Some adversity feels like training. Some adversity feels like it tears your life in half. Learning to swim shook me, but it didn't redefine my world. Losing my father did.

I've said that I've never met a great person who didn't have a story of great pain. For me, that pain has a name, a voice, a presence I still miss: my father.

His death forced me to see life differently. Nothing places life in perspective like death. It confronts you with a truth we all know but rarely live by: there is an end to this. Our time is limited. How we live, how we love, how we lead, and how we impact cannot be delayed to "one day" forever.

When my father died, it wasn't just a date on a calendar. It was a line drawn through my story—before and after. Before, I assumed I had time. After, I understood I had an assignment.

For a while, grief felt like it owned me. I wrestled with questions: Why now? Why him? Why this way? But slowly, the questions began to change. Instead of only asking, "Why did this happen?" I started asking, "Who can I become because this happened?"

That's when this truth became real:

Adversity will always be your greatest adversary until you choose to embrace it as your greatest ally.

The death of my father did not end my story. In many ways, it began the life of purpose I now live. Where his life stopped, something in me started. My urgency sharpened. My sense of stewardship over my gift deepened. My message gained weight.

My healing came as I helped others heal. As I spoke life, inspired, and challenged people, the words that flowed through me started working in me. What I was pouring out left a residue on my own soul. Serving others didn't erase my grief, but it transformed what grief did to me.

As I write this book, I can't help but fight back tears as I dedicate it to my late father, Cornelius Royal Glasgow. Dad, I love you and I miss you deeply. As I grow and evolve, I realize I don't just miss your presence; I miss the opportunity to show you the return on your investment—to show you that I became someone you could be proud of, someone whose life proves that yours mattered. I believe that was your greatest desire: to know your life made a difference.

Today, every time I stand in my calling, I know your mission still lives on through your son. So even with a heavy heart, tears on my face, and moments of loneliness or doubt, I still execute with fire— because I know I am finishing not only what you started, but also what you would have wanted to finish and simply didn't have enough time to complete.

Pops, let's go to work. I'm restating the same promise I whispered as you lay in that casket: Don't worry. I've got us.

This is what it means when I say adversity can become an ally. It doesn't mean what happened was good. It means you refuse to let what happened be wasted.

HOW YOU INTERPRET ADVERSITY DETERMINES WHAT IT BECOMES

There's a mindset shift I want to offer you:

Stop obsessing over wishing, wanting, and hoping for your adversity to change—and start discovering how your adversity is trying to change you.

Because:

- Adversity misinterpreted leads to lifelong misery. When you see adversity only as evidence that you're cursed, forgotten, or less than, you carry it like identity instead of treating it as information.
- Adversity embraced can become your greatest ally. When you decide not to ask just "Why me?" but "Who can I become?" adversity becomes raw material for transformation.

I'm sensitive to the fact that some adversity is unspeakably painful. There are things people have walked through that I will never justify or minimize. But I refuse to let those things be the final authors of our lives. Yes, adversity may have impacted you. No, it doesn't have to define you.

ADVERSITY AS RESISTANCE ON THE WAY TO REWARD

One of my favorite communicators Mike McClure Jr. once said, "Adversity is the way we define the resistance necessary for the reward." I loved that so much I wrote it down.

When you chase something bigger than where you are now, you will meet resistance. That resistance is not proof you're on the wrong path. It's proof that what you're going after requires you to grow, stretch, and execute on a different level.

Adversity, then, is often evidence that you've outgrown your current capacity and are being invited into more.

It is also an awakening. Adversity disrupts your picture of how you thought life would go. When that picture shatters, you suddenly have the opportunity to build a new one—often one you never believed was possible before.

Adversity can awaken you to a higher position, a deeper potential, and a clearer understanding of who you truly are versus who you've believed yourself to be.

WHAT ADVERSITY REVEALS

If you're willing to lean in instead of just trying to escape, adversity can become one of your greatest teachers. Here are a few of the ways it does that.

1. ADVERSITY REVEALS CHARACTER FLAWS

We don't really know where the cracks in our character are until something presses on them. Adversity exposes the places where we react instead of respond, where we run instead of stand, where we cling to ego instead of humility.

Seeing those flaws is not about shame. It's about clarity. Once you see them, you can take ownership and begin to grow. Transformation often requires that something hidden be brought to the surface, and adversity is one of the most efficient—though uncomfortable—ways that happens.

2. ADVERSITY FILTERS AND FORGES RELATIONSHIPS

Adversity will show you who is really with you. I know who is for me by who stays when I'm going through something that doesn't benefit them.

Sometimes adversity shows up not because of what it's doing to you, but because of what it's doing for you—shaking loose relationships, patterns, and attachments you don't have the courage to release. It filters out those who only love your strength and forges deeper connection with those who can also love you in weakness.

Some of the most meaningful relationships in my life were forged in the fires of adversity. When things "hit the floor," you find out what people are truly made of.

3. ADVERSITY DEEPENS COMMITMENT

Commitment that is never tested cannot be trusted. You don't really know how committed you are—to a vision, a relationship, a calling— until adversity hits it.

Adversity forces you to decide: Are you in this as long as it's convenient, or are you in this because it's who you are? It strips away the illusion of convenient commitment and invites you into something deeper, more resilient, and more authentic.

CHOOSING HOW YOU WILL RESPOND

You may not have chosen the adversity that showed up in your life. You didn't schedule the diagnosis, the loss, the betrayal, the layoff, the disappointment. But you still have a choice.

You can spend the rest of your life trying to move the rock—or you can realize the rock is moving you.

The question I want to invite you into is this:

What if this adversity isn't happening to you, but for you?

Not in a way that denies the pain or dismisses the injustice, but in a way that asks:

- What is this adversity revealing about me?
- What is it removing from my life that I didn't have the courage to release?
- Who am I becoming because of what I've walked through?

You may not be able to change what happened, but you have immense power over what it produces in you.

Adversity will either become your greatest adversary or your greatest ally. That shift doesn't happen when the circumstances change. It happens when you change.

And when you choose to let adversity refine you instead of define you, pain stops being the period at the end of your story—and becomes the comma that introduces the next sentence of your purpose.

Adversity may refine you, but it was never meant to replace your fire. Its role is to strengthen the hands that carry it, not to steal the flame itself. In the final chapter, we're going to talk about that fire—how to recognize it, how to protect it, and how to stay connected to it long after the applause fades and the storm passes. Because once you understand adversity as an ally, the next question is simple: how do you keep your fire burning in a world that keeps trying to put it out?

CHAPTER 14

STAYING CONNECTED TO YOUR FIRE

THERE IS A moment in every journey where the question is no longer, Do I have a dream? but, Do I still have a fire? You can have vision, strategy, habits, and even results, and still feel like something inside you has quietly dimmed. That inner flame—the conviction, joy, and sense of assignment that once felt unshakeable—can start to flicker under the weight of delays, detours, and disappointments.

This chapter is about that flame. It is about staying unstoppable—not because life never hits you, but because you refuse to let what hits you hard also live in you long. Staying connected to your fire is less about hype and more about one decision you will have to make over and over again for the rest of your life: the decision to release disappointments quickly so they cannot become your identity.

When I talk about "your fire," I'm not talking about a personality type or a temporary surge of motivation. I'm not talking about the loudest person in the room or the one who can post the most inspirational quotes. Your fire is the intersection of three things:

- **Your conviction:** what you know you are called to.
- **Your compassion:** who you care about so deeply that it moves you to act.
- **Your clarity:** the growing awareness of how your gifts are meant to serve.

That fire shows up in different ways. For some, it looks like boldness and visibility. For others, it looks like quiet consistency, building and serving in rooms that never make it to social media. But at its core, your fire is that internal yes—the part of you that says, I was created for this. I cannot sit this out and still be true to who I am.

Here's the tension: fire doesn't just go out because of failure. It often dims because of unreleased disappointment. It's not just what happened—it's what we start believing about ourselves because it happened.

Earlier in this book, we talked about adversity, burnout, and the danger of letting shame turn reflection into punishment instead of clarity. We talked about patterns and undercurrents, hamster wheels and underthesurface winds that keep pushing the same waves into your life. We talked about how disappointment, if it lingers long enough, can start whispering stories about your worth and your future.

Disappointment is sneaky. It doesn't always show up as a dramatic breakdown. More often, it shows up as:

- The opportunity you were sure would come through, but didn't.
- The relationship you thought would be safe, but wasn't.
- The season where you did everything "right" and still didn't get the outcome you prayed for.

If you're not careful, that disappointment doesn't just sit in a moment—it starts building a narrative.

- "Maybe I'm not as called as I thought."
- "Maybe I should shrink my expectations."
- "Maybe this dream was naïve."

That is how people go from on fire to just functioning. They don't stop caring. They just stop believing with the same intensity because disappointment has been sitting in their chest for too long, unaddressed.

I learned this the hard way. There were seasons where I was still on stages, still delivering, still impacting lives, but on the inside I was wrestling with closed doors that didn't make sense, partnerships that fell apart, and personal losses that left me wondering if God had accidentally skipped over some details in my story. I was effective, but I wasn't as present. The gift was working, but the fire behind it was flickering.

Disappointment, when you hold onto it, doesn't just steal your joy. It slowly rearranges your identity. It moves you from "I faced something hard" to "I must not be enough."

THE WEIGHTLESS WALK AND DISAPPOINTMENT

In the chapter on unshakable confidence, we talked about power as a weightless walk—learning to release entitlement through gratitude, ego through humility, and offense through forgiveness so you can move freely in who you are. Staying connected to your fire is that same principle applied specifically to disappointment.

Think about disappointment again as a brick. Every time something doesn't turn out the way you expected, life hands you a brick. You may not have asked for it, but it's in your hands. You have two options:

- You can carry it—rehearsing the story, replaying the pain, letting it shape how you see yourself.
- Or you can build with it—allowing it to become context, wisdom, and compassion that fuels your calling instead of smothering it.

The Weightless Walk gives us three tools for releasing those bricks quickly:

1. Gratitude – shifting your focus from what you lost to what you still have and what you gained in wisdom.
2. Humility – admitting you are not in control of every outcome, but you are responsible for your response.
3. Forgiveness – refusing to keep carrying the weight of what they did, what you did, or what never happened the way you planned.

When you practice these three intentionally, disappointment doesn't get to become a permanent resident. It becomes a visitor that comes, teaches you something, and then leaves.

RELEASE, RESET, REENGAGE

I want to make this painfully practical, because staying connected to your fire will not be an abstract concept—you will need a rhythm you can run to when life punches you in the chest.

I call it Release, Reset, ReEngage.

1. RELEASE: TELL THE TRUTH AND LET IT GO

Releasing disappointment starts with honesty. Not church answers. Not "I'm fine." Real honesty.

Ask yourself:

- What actually hurt me here?
- What did I expect that didn't happen?
- What am I afraid this disappointment means about me?

Write it down. Say it out loud. Pray it. Take it to God, to a counselor, to a trusted friend who can handle the full weight of your truth. You cannot release what you keep pretending doesn't exist.

Then, choose forgiveness.

- Forgive the person who dropped the ball.
- Forgive the system that didn't see you.
- Forgive yourself for what you didn't know, didn't do, or didn't see coming.

Forgiveness is not saying it was okay. It is saying, "This happened, but it will not have the final say in who I become." It is taking the brick out of your backpack and putting it on the ground.

You may have to do this more than once. Some disappointments are heavier than others. That's okay. Keep putting the brick down.

2. RESET: REMEMBER YOUR STANCE IN THE CYCLE

We broke down the word circumstance earlier—circum meaning cycle, stance meaning posture or position. Your circumstance is your stance in a cycle. When disappointment hits, your first instinct will be to stare at the cycle—what keeps happening, what went wrong again.

Resetting is about shifting your attention back to your stance. Ask yourself:

- Who am I, even here?
- What values am I refusing to betray, even in this frustration?
- What truth about my identity do I need to rehearse louder than this disappointment?

Maybe that truth is: "I am not my last result. I am not my last no. I am not my last failure. I am someone who learns, adapts, and rises." Maybe it's a scripture that reminds you your value is not up for negotiation.

Resetting is where gratitude and humility meet. Gratitude says, "Even here, I still have breath, possibility, and purpose." Humility says, "I don't see the full picture yet, but I will keep walking in obedience, not just in outcomes."

This is also where you revisit your why. The story of Cha Sasoon, the Korean grandmother who failed her driver's test 960 times and kept showing up, wasn't about driving—it was about purpose. She wanted freedom. She wanted to take her grandchildren places. When purpose is clear, rejection loses its power to define you. Resetting is you choosing to see your disappointment through the lens of your assignment, not the other way around.

3. REENGAGE: TAKE ONE ALIGNED STEP

Staying connected to your fire will always bring you back to action. Not frantic, performative action. Aligned action.

After you release and reset, ask:

- What is one small, aligned step I can take today that agrees with who I'm becoming?
- How can I show up—imperfectly, but fully—right where I am?

Sometimes that step is sending the email. Sometimes it's resting on purpose so you don't burn out. Sometimes it's scheduling the counseling session. Sometimes it's picking the mic back up after a hard season and telling the truth about where you've been.

Remember the rock that wouldn't move—the story of the boy who spent years pushing a boulder at his grandfather's request. The rock never budged. But when he finally stepped back, his body had changed. His strength had grown. The rock was never the point. The point was who he became while he was pushing.

Reengaging after disappointment is you choosing to push again—not because you're sure the rock will move this time, but because you are sure you are not done becoming.

FIRE AND THE HABITS THAT GUARD IT

In the previous chapter, we talked about purposeful preparation, quiet contemplation, and consistent commitment as daily habits that help you build a life you love. Those habits were never just about productivity. They were always about protection—protecting your peace, your alignment, and your fire.

- Purposeful preparation helps you decide what matters before the day starts throwing distractions and unexpected hits at you. When disappointment shows up, that preparation keeps you from giving your whole identity to one moment.
- Quiet contemplation gives you space to process pain before it turns into permanent narratives. It's where you bring disappointment into the light with God, with yourself, with the truth, instead of letting it grow mold in the dark.
- Consistent commitment—your microkeeps and nonnegotiables—reminds you that even when the big thing didn't happen, you are still someone who shows up. You're still honoring your health, your heart, and your mission one small act at a time.

These habits don't eliminate disappointment. They reduce its ability to hijack your whole life.

A WORD TO THE ONES CARRYING QUIET FIRES

Before we close, I want to speak directly to a few of you.

To the leader who feels unseen…

You are the one who shows up early, stays late, carries the weight no one else wants, and still goes home wondering if any of it really matters. You pour into your team, your family, your community, and yet there are nights when you lie awake and think, "Who pours into me?" You've had ideas overlooked, sacrifices forgotten, and loyalty taken for granted. And somewhere along the way, disappointment started whispering, "Maybe I'm invisible. Maybe I'm replaceable."

If that's you, hear me clearly: your fire is not defined by who sees it—it is defined by Who sent it. The lack of applause has never been proof of a lack of impact. Heaven has receipts for seeds you've sown that no one else even knows about. Staying connected to your fire in this season will mean releasing the disappointment of not being recognized as quickly as it lands, so it doesn't turn into resentment. Let gratitude remind you of the privilege of serving. Let humility keep you open to feedback without shrinking your worth. Let forgiveness free you from the need to be understood by everyone you lead. Keep leading like someone's breakthrough is attached to your obedience—because it is.

To the one rebuilding after divorce, betrayal, or heartbreak…

You didn't just lose a relationship. You lost a version of your future you had already started living in your mind. You lost traditions, rhythms, maybe even a shared friend circle or faith community. And if we're honest, you lost some trust in yourself—trust in your discernment, your judgment, your ability to choose well. Disappointment in others has quietly turned into disappointment in you. You might be asking, "How did I miss this? What does this say about me?"

I need you to know: what happened to you is not who you are. Your fire may feel fragile right now, but it is not gone. Staying connected to it will look like releasing the disappointment in layers—not pretending you're fine, but refusing to let this chapter rename you. Release the shame that keeps replaying every red flag you didn't act on. Reset your stance by remembering that you are still worthy of love, respect, and partnership that honors who you are becoming. Reengage by taking small, brave steps—healing conversations, counseling, saying yes to community again, allowing yourself to dream of a life that's not built around the wound but around your wholeness. Your heart can hold both the grief of what ended and the fire for what's still possible.

To the dreamer who feels late to the party...

Maybe you're looking at your age, your bank account, your responsibilities and thinking, "If this was really supposed to happen, wouldn't it have happened by now?" Social media has you scrolling through highlight reels of people who seem younger, further along, better resourced. You've survived enough delays and detours that disappointment has started dressing itself up as "realism." You still have a dream—but you've put an expiration date on it.

Let me tell you something that shifted me: timing can delay a dream, but only agreement can kill it. Staying connected to your fire in this season means refusing to agree with the lie that you are late. You are right on time for the version of you that can actually carry what you're asking for. Release the disappointment of the timelines you created in your head. Reset by asking, "Given who I am today, what is my next faithful step?" not, "How quickly can I catch up?" Reengage your dream in ways that honor your current season—maybe that means building in the margins, moving slower but deeper, focusing on mastery instead of speed. You're not behind; you're being prepared differently.

To the one who's just tired…

You're not in a scandal. You're not in a crisis. You're just tired of always having to be the strong one. Tired of stretching every dollar, every hour, every ounce of emotional energy. Tired of starting over. Tired of hoping again. You love God, you love people, you believe in purpose—but lately, your strongest prayer has been, "Lord, I'm exhausted."

If that's you, your fire doesn't need more pressure; it needs more protection. Staying unstoppable for you will look less like doing more and more like giving yourself permission to rest without calling it weakness. Release the disappointment you feel toward your own limits—the frustration that you can't carry everything the way you used to. Reset your stance by honoring your humanity as much as your assignment. Reengage, not by piling on new commitments, but by returning to the few nonnegotiables that actually keep your heart alive: real rest, honest relationships, and time in the Presence that reminds you you're loved before you're useful. Sometimes the most faithfilled thing you can do is take a breath, take a break, and then take the next step.

Whoever you are, wherever you find yourself as you read this, I want you to hear this one more time: your fire is still there. It may be covered in ashes of disappointment, but embers are still burning. And if you will release quickly what was never meant to define you, reset your stance in the truth of who you are, and reengage your life from that place—you will not just finish this book inspired. You will walk into your next season ignited.

STAYING UNSTOPPABLE IS A DECISION

I need you to understand this: unstoppable does not mean untouched. Unstoppable means you have decided that nothing you face gets to turn you into someone you are not.

You will have seasons of grief. You will have seasons where doors slam in your face. You will have seasons where your own choices cost you more than you expected. Being unstoppable doesn't mean you never cry. It means you don't build your home in the place that broke you.

- You may bend, but you will not break.
- You may pause, but you will not live in paralysis.
- You may hurt, but you will not hand your identity over to the hurt.

Staying connected to your fire is a thousand quiet decisions:

- To forgive one more time.
- To tell the truth about where you are without quitting on who you are.
- To rest before you collapse so you can keep carrying your assignment with integrity.
- To honor the gift God put in you, even when you feel overlooked by people.

There will be days when all you can pray is, "God, keep my heart from hardening here." That prayer alone is a way of staying connected to your fire. A hard heart can't burn. A guarded, honest heart can.

YOUR DASH, YOUR FIRE, YOUR LEGACY

Earlier, we talked about the dash on your tombstone—the small line between the day you arrived and the day you leave. That dash is your life. And your life, when everything else is stripped away, will be remembered by one word: impact.

No one will stand at your funeral and talk about every disappointment that tried to take you out. They will talk about the fire you carried and what that fire did in them.

They will remember:

- The way you kept showing up when quitting would have been easier.
- The way you apologized when you were wrong and didn't let shame keep you from growing.
- The way you loved people deeply, even after being hurt.
- The way you lived with urgency, not because you were afraid of dying, but because you were committed to actually living.

When my father died, my world split into "before" and "after." His death forced me to understand that time is not promised and that impact is the only thing that truly remains. Every time I stand on a stage or sit with a leader and help them see themselves differently, I know I am carrying his fire forward. His life poured into mine; my life now pours into others. That is legacy.

As you close this book, I want you to remember something we've been saying in different ways from the very beginning: You made it—now make something meaningful out of your life. Not a perfect life. A whole one. A life where your purpose and potential are realized, your norms are healthy, your habits are aligned, and your disappointments are released quickly enough that they cannot rewrite your identity.

You will not always feel on fire. But you will always have access to the spark.

Every time you choose reflection without shame over selfattack…
Every time you choose ownership over excuses…
Every time you choose vision over validation…
Every time you choose fulfillment over chasing…

Every time you choose gratitude, humility, and forgiveness over entitlement, ego, and offense…
Every time you choose to release, reset, and reengage after disappointment…

You are stoking the fire again.

If your mind can conceive this, and your heart will believe it, your hands can create a life, impact, love, and legacy that your younger self never even knew was possible. So here is my final invitation to you:

- Stay honest enough to feel.
- Stay humble enough to learn.
- Stay brave enough to release quickly what was never meant to define you.
- Stay committed enough to keep showing up, especially for you.

Because as long as there is breath in your body, there is still fire in your story.

Stay connected to it. Let it light the way for you—and for everyone who will one day say, "I didn't just hear their message. I watched their life burn with purpose, and it gave me permission to find my own."

ACKNOWLEDGMENTS

First, I give all honor, glory, and gratitude to the Lord Jesus Christ for His love, grace, and ultimate sacrifice for me. Without His hand on my life, this book—and the man I am still becoming—would not exist.

To my wife, Shelly Glasgow, thank you for your support, sacrifice, and the countless unseen ways you hold our home together so I can pour into the world. Your steadiness has been an anchor in seasons where my assignment demanded more than my strength felt able to carry.

To my mother, Annelle Glasgow, thank you for your prayers, your love, and the kind of covering that cannot be measured in words. Your faith planted seeds in me long before I had language for the calling on my life.

To my sister, Cordine Glasgow, your support and dedication have meant more than you know. Thank you for believing in me, standing with me, and reminding me that I never had to walk this journey alone.

To George, my designer and creative partner in bringing this book to life, thank you for stewarding this message with excellence. You didn't just design pages; you helped build a home for these words to live in.

To my children, Khila, Elion, and Chris—you are my why. Your lives are a constant reminder of the legacy I want to build, the cycles I want to break, and the standard I want to set. You inspire my work, my growth, and my commitment to becoming the man you deserve to see.

To Alton Voss, my dear friend and brother, whose own journey and resilience continually inspire me to be my best and make an impact in the world—I cannot wait for the world to hear your story.

To everyone who has ever sat in a room where I've spoken, shared a story with me, or trusted me with your pain and your dreams—thank you. Your honesty and your courage echo through these pages.

ABOUT THE AUTHOR

JOVAN GLASGOW is an influencer of change, entrepreneur, speaker, and human transformation expert who helps high-performing individuals and leaders do more than succeed on paper—he helps them become whole. Drawing from his own journey through adversity, Jovan equips people to rewire their beliefs, break destructive patterns, and build lives and organizations that are both high-performing and deeply aligned.

As a sought-after keynote speaker and performance coach, Jovan works with executives, teams, and high-capacity professionals who are tired of living in quiet misalignment. His work focuses on shifting inner narratives, transforming culture from the inside out, and creating sustainable results that do not cost people their peace, identity, or purpose.

Born and raised in Antigua and Barbuda, Jovan now lives in Dallas, Texas, where he continues to write, speak, and develop resources that help people go deeper than motivation and into true transformation.

To connect with Jovan, inquire about booking, or explore events and additional resources, email **deeperthanmotivation@gmail.com** or visit **www.iamjovanglasgow.com**.